WOW!

that's what i call service!

by
Don Hales and Derek Williams

Ecademy Press
6 Woodland Rise, Penryn, Cornwall TR10 8QD, UK
info@ecademy-press.com • www.ecademy-press.com

Cover Design by Martin Coote
Book Design & Typsetting by AuthorHouse
Set in Minion Pro 12 on 18pt

ISBN: 978-1-905823-16-1
ISBN: 1-905823-16-9

First published 06/14/07 by Ecademy Press

Printed and Bound by:
Lightning Source in the UK and USA

Printed on acid-free paper from managed forests. This book is printed on demand, so no copies will be remaindered or pulped.

To Don's grandsons, Finlay and Joseph,
and
Derek's granddaughter, Lilly,
customers of the future!

Contents

WOW!
that's what i call service!

What's it all about?

Every experience is a learning opportunity.

We can learn a huge amount from making mistakes or from other people's mistakes.

But if we really aspire to be the best then we have to learn from the best.

These stories are about some of the very best customer service from businesses in the UK (with just a few examples from other countries).

The stories come from two sources:-

1. The National Customer Service Awards.

   Don Hales has been organiser and chairman of judges for the National Customer Service Awards since 2000. He has inspected the written entries and seen the presentations from literally thousands of individuals and businesses covering every sector of business in the UK.

The stories from Don provide a fascinating insight into what makes some of these businesses tick and how they have achieved greatness.

2. The WOW! Awards

Derek Williams created The WOW! Awards in 1999. His mission is to raise standards of customer service in the UK to the point that visitors from Florida say, 'WOW! Have you seen what a great job the Brits are doing?'

Nominations for The WOW! Awards have to come from genuine third party customers. Individuals and businesses cannot enter themselves.

Many of The WOW! Awards stories come straight from the customer and are largely unedited. Some might be quite short or even appear quite ordinary. But in every case a customer felt 'WOW'ed! enough to make a nomination. And that is what every business should be aspiring to.

The greatest surprise with The WOW! Awards is the enthusiasm that customers have for making nominations. And in many instances, customers have gone out of their way and incurred extra expense to present a certificate to the winning businesses.

Individuals

For us, this is probably the most important section of the book.

It will always be individuals who make the difference.

Although, as customers, we might first select a business based on its brand name and its reputation we will very soon start to make judgments based on the service that we received from individuals.

Individuals have the power to make or break the relationship. All of the time and money that has been invested in development and marketing could be completely wasted if someone in the front line is not able to meet our expectations. We firmly believe that the front liners are the most important people in the organisation. And the role of management should be to support those front liners in the job that they do.

We are also great believers in 'catching people doing things right!'

In many businesses, management time is dominated with catching people doing things wrong. Someone gets called into the manager's office because they have failed to hit the target or a customer has complained.

How much better it would be if the majority of management time was taken up with catching people doing things right. Some people might never have been to Head Office or met the directors of the company. Wouldn't it be great if they were called in occasionally to be given praise?

And when we start to catch people doing things right that reinforces the behaviour that we are all looking for.

That Perfect Day

For many ladies and, indeed, gentleman, their wedding day will be one of the most memorable of their lives. Weddings are, of course, very big business and sometimes in the midst of all the arrangements in the weeks and months (and, in some cases, years) leading up to the great event the commercial interests of those providing the various services can be less than in sympathy with the occasion itself.

Not so for weddings organised by Jane Fair, the wedding organiser at the Holiday Inn, Doncaster – part of the QMH UK hotel group. Since joining the hotel in 2002, Jane has established a tremendous reputation for ensuring smooth, carefree arrangements for hundreds of brides. Remembering her own wedding day, she sets out with the sole intention of ensuring that for every couple their wedding will be the most memorable day of their life.

Although contracted to fairly standard office hours, Jane takes a very flexible approach to her working week. She will often work late into the evening and at weekends to meet customers at times most convenient to them and, of course, she attends all the weddings – even building her own holidays around them.

She handles every kind of wedding ceremony from traditional to modern, religious and non-religious, ones with a service and those without, Asian, Jewish and more recently including civil partnerships. Jane studies the needs and goes to fantastic lengths to ensure that perfect day every time. The case of civil partnerships illustrates the point. As soon as she knew that these were about to take place, she researched the background both in the UK and in other countries, especially America, where they had been taking place for some time, in order to be able to offer them as soon as they were legally available.

When discussing a potential wedding with a couple at the start of her relationship with them, Jane never pushes them into deciding to use her facilities. She believes that they will know if the venue choice is right for them. And if so, she swings into action.

Diplomacy is high on Jane's list of required skills for her role as she often has to preside over family differences and she tactfully glides the decision in favour of the bride and groom's best interest. Jane's aim is to make every couple feel that theirs is the only wedding she is handling, whereas she actually organises about 120 a year.

As a hotel professional, Jane has worked in every department at the hotel and, on the day, she will assist in the kitchen or bar, if the need arises. She obtains fantastic co-operation from her hotel colleagues, as they know how important the day is to the customers and how hard Jane works to deliver the perfect day.

Incidentally Jane has not neglected the commercial side of her business. By putting the needs of the bride and groom first, she has built up an unenviable record as a wedding organiser par excellence. As a result of her hard work, attention to detail and total care for the customer, she has increased the number of weddings per year at her venue by 400%

and the revenue by 600% and she now also advises other wedding advisors in her group so that they can emulate her success.

Amongst the unusual requests that Jane receives are to replicate weddings of famous celebrities and to provide special adornments, such as pink carpets and 'a dress like Jordan's'. On a more practical level she ensures that even the weather cannot spoil the great day and always ensures that there is a contingency plan for outdoor events. In this regard, a Hindu ceremony involving a ritual fire caused problems with health and safety when she was working on her 'indoor contingency plan' and the hotel fire alarm system also needed to be considered but nothing deters Jane from finding a solution.

On the big day itself, she always has emergency supplies of hankies, note pads and pens, safety pins and chalk. She has quickly fished wedding rings from the linings of the Best Man's jacket and even taken lessons in hypnotherapy for calming techniques to help her customers.

Obtaining positive feedback from every couple is another of Jane's achievements but she knows that she is unlikely to get repeat business from her immediate customers. Her business is built on recommendation and reputation and there are future customers and parents of customers in every wedding party and that is largely where her reputation is built.

Another wedding organiser's story:

A year or so back we had another wedding organiser in the finals of the National Customer Service Awards with a great story to tell. On one occasion the bride arrived with her family at the rather grand Renaissance Hotel in central London, planning to have a big dinner party with her family on the eve of her wedding.

The bride was sharing a room with her grandmother to whom she was particularly close – just as well in view of what was to happen! Just before they went down to dinner the grandmother decided to look for somewhere safe to hang the beautiful bridal gown. She chose a convenient apparatus that was protruding from the ceiling in the middle of the room. It was in fact the sprinkler head, part of the premises' fire alarm system.

All seemed well as they left the room but while they were dining with the rest of the family, the weight of the dress gradually pulled down on the sprinkler head, eventually causing it to discharge gallons of water that flooded the room.

When the bride returned later that night, she found the room awash and her wedding dress, most of the wedding presents, the place names for the reception and many other important items for the wedding reception all floating in the water and all completely destroyed.

Needless to say the bride was distraught and the wedding dress was her biggest problem.

Our wedding organiser swung into action and was able to find solutions for most of the problems, including finding members of the hotel staff with fine handwriting to write the place names.

Replacing the wedding dress remained the biggest challenge. With just hours to go, she stormed into a bridal gown dressmaker in town that had supplied many of her brides in the past. She saw a beautiful gown that would be just right for her distressed bride, hanging proudly in a corner. 'I'll take that,' she said, grabbing it off the hook. 'You can't have that,' cried the dressmaker, 'that's for (naming a B list celebrity) who's getting married in three days time.' 'My bride needs it now' replied our heroine, who swept out before any further argument could take place.

The wedding went ahead and the bride looked stunning. A few days later the same dress appeared in all the national papers when our celebrity got married with just a handful of people knowing that it had been used a few days earlier.

This is another great example of a customer service star going the extra mile when the chips are down.

Catching People Doing Things Right – Ladbrokes

In 2004, Ladbrokes took a real lead in using The WOW! Awards to help them improve their customer service. For a period of one month they ran a poster campaign in all 2000 of their betting shops. Alongside each of the posters was a little feedback form inviting customers to make a nomination.

During a period of one month, Ladbrokes received 460 nominations. Of these, 70 were submitted to the judges of The WOW! Awards. 20 received individual certificates. And Alexis Simpson was put forward as a finalist in The National Customer Service Awards.

Nominations for Alexis and her shop in Union Street, Aberdeen were received from Jorge Herrera, Miguel Feijoo, Graham Rennie (on behalf of 5 other people), Olive Hutcheon, Mark Fraser, Mr T Ewen, Scott Colegate, Eduardo Moreno, and Mr M Flanagan.

Comments about the team at Aberdeen included:-

> "I would like to nominate Alexis Simpson for the way she has changed the concept of betting shops. It is a pleasure going into her shop. Her staff are so friendly and helpful."

"Every Saturday she puts a table out with rolls, biscuits, tea and coffee. All she asks for is a donation for a local cancer charity whether it is 5p or £5, it does not matter."

"On big race days she makes costumes for all staff and herself and has photos with the staff and customers together. On these days she organises raffles, has the likes of homemade stovies (a traditional Scottish dish of minced meat and potatoes) or Chile which again is only a donation. I personally am in ill-health and cannot eat spicy food. Alexis actually brought in a slice of sirloin steak and a couple of crispy Glasgow rolls. She cut the steak and put it on the rolls for me and it was really appreciated."

"If you want to see 21st century bookmakers at their best then visit your shop at 198 Union St. It has to be seen to be believed! I never thought that I would look forward to a visit to the bookmakers so much. But thanks to Alexis and her staff I have a new circle of friends. Alexis is a jewel in the Ladbroke's crown."

"I do not speak good English but Alexis Simpson helped me every day. She checked my bills and helped me fill in forms. She has good time for everybody and understanding mostly. When she does cooking, I get some always to take home to my friend. I have coffee always even if she is busy and also she tells me to take my tablets."

When it came to the judging of the National Customer Service Awards, Alexis made a phenomenal presentation.

She had made a video about the things that she does in her shop. It clearly showed how she makes costumes for all her people and a buffet for her customers. She organises charity collections and helps customers in all sorts of small ways.

One of her customers tells how he always comes back to Aberdeen from England if there is a big race meeting on. The atmosphere at the Aberdeen shop is so good and no other betting shop treats its customers so well.

Alexis pays for the costumes from her own pocket.

Alexis pays for the buffet from her own pocket.

And Alexis made the video herself.

In my presentations around the world, I have shown people the Alexis video and posed this question. If you were one of the directors of Ladbrokes watching that film, how would you feel?

"Proud" and "humbled" are the two words that most often come back as the reply.

Ladbrokes continued the programme for 2005 and this time The WOW! Awards judges selected Ruben Casco as a finalist.

Ruben went on to win The WOW! Awards final at the National Customer Service Awards. Although he is only 24 years old, Ruben was nominated by 51 punters at his shop in Mill Hill, London.

Ladbrokes Retail Operations Director Dominic Matthews said: "Ruben consistently delivers the kind of customer service we endeavour to offer in all of our shops on a daily basis.

In fact he is a shining example to all who strive to deliver positive customer service no matter what industry they are in.

Winning a national award like this is a tremendous achievement - particularly as all of the nominations came from shop customers, who took the time to support him. We are very proud of him."

Among the outstanding achievements listed by Ruben's supporters was his decision to drive a customer, whose car had broken down, to Bristol on his day off. A return journey of 240 miles! And he helped another to an osteopath after he developed a bad back.

Shop Manager Steven Halliday said: "Ruben is permanently happy and the customers see this and immediately warm to him. He's a natural."

Nominations include one from Joe Kinnear, manager of Nottingham Forest football club, who says, "Great team! Keep it up! Simply the best."

And Neil Freeman had this to say. "I am a manager with William Hill. The service in this shop is top-class. And I would be happy to have any of the staff working for me."

Michael Patsalides told us, "Ruben is always cheerful and willing to help in any way he can. A real asset to any company."

For the year to May 2006, Ladbrokes were so pleased with the results from The WOW! Awards nominations that they ran the programme throughout the year. During this period they received 1752 nominations!

Fiona Critchall from Gosport was one of the winners. She was nominated by Ted Munden.

Ted was a regular visitor to Fiona's shop. But when Ted broke his arm he was unable to make the journey to the shop. Fiona heard about this from one of Ted's friends and made arrangements to collect him from his home and bring him into the shop so that he could places bets.

Fiona also helped Ted with shopping and to get to a hospital appointment.

The first Fiona knew about this nomination was when we contacted her to let her know that she had been selected as a finalist in the 2006 National Customer Service Awards. Unfortunately, Ted had since passed away but his nomination is a lasting reminder of his gratitude to Fiona.

The WOW! Awards has helped Ladbrokes to do something quite extraordinary. They now catch people doing things right! And doing things that management might never have known about if it wasn't for those little customer nominations forms.

Ladbrokes have succeeded in making The WOW! Awards an integral part of their customer service development. But this would not have happened without the vision and the leadership of their management. In particular, Margaret Conlon, Customer Services Project Manager, deserves a special mention.

Not only did Margaret ensure that Ladbrokes achieved the success that they deserved, she has also helped to advise many other companies about how they could use The WOW! Awards with their people and with their customers.

Thank you, Margaret. You are a star!

Far Away Places – BA Holidays

When you are far away from home and something goes wrong with your holiday, you can feel isolated and frustrated. This is why British

Airways Holidays provide a 24/7 365 days of the year hotline to sort out any problems that their customers might encounter. They work on the basis that monetary compensation after the holiday, to make good the promise shortfall, is not only very expensive to the company, but also far less than satisfactory for the customer as you cannot grab back the time to recreate the holiday experience which is what the customer originally wanted.

Their approach has been to solve the problem as quickly as possible so that the customer can enjoy the holiday they wanted and paid for. A typical call might be from a couple, just arrived at their destination in Florida, who find that they have not got the sea view room they booked and the hotel is not proving very helpful. It may be 2 a.m. in the morning when the call comes through to the UK but the team is on hand immediately to set about finding a solution.

The team is skilled at resolving these issues as quickly as possible and they have a great record for recovering situations when things go wrong as can happen in a business of this nature.

They also have overseas customers visiting the UK for business or pleasure from various countries, including the United States of America and it was one such customer that really drew out the best in Charlotte (or Charley) Lawrence who won the Young Customer Service Professional of the Year in 2005.

The customer in question was an elderly but active American gentleman who was visiting London to see the sights and to buy works of art from some of the capital's galleries. Unfortunately whilst he was in town, he suffered a heart attack and found himself seriously ill in hospital in a country where he knew no one.

No one that is, except Charley. As soon as she heard of his plight, Charley set about sorting out his situation. The customer's only living adult relative was his daughter who lived in Israel. Charley contacted the daughter and arranged her flights and accommodation to visit her father. As she had a young family, the daughter could not fly immediately as she had to make arrangements for her children.

Charley kept in touch with the customer on the telephone, ringing several times a day to tell him of the arrangements she had made, including sorting out everything with his hotel, rescuing his personal effects and, most importantly, looking after the artworks. She knew that the customer looked forward to her calls, as she was his only contact in town. She always chatted on the phone to him about his progress and his grandchildren and generally kept his spirits up until his daughter could arrive.

One day she and a senior colleague even journeyed to London to visit the customer in hospital. The time and genuine interest she provided for this customer turned what could have been a completely disastrous experience into a positive one. The customer was eventually sufficiently recovered in order to fly home to the States. Charley again made all the flight arrangements as appropriate for his condition and contacted him once he reached home and made sure that he and his treasured artworks were safe and secure.

Charley really pulled out all the stops out here. The customer went as far as saying that he really did not know what would have happened to him in his time of despair without her help and concern.

No wonder sorting out another room booking gone wrong is something that Charley can sort out with patience, understanding and humour. She knows what it is like when something seriously goes wrong – and she has handled customers' problems during 9/11, the Tsunami and 7/7 – and rises to the challenge every time.

The Human Whirlwind –
Basil Martinez, Gingham's Coffee Shop

Basil Martinez is a young man who clears tables at a little coffee shop called Gingham's at the end of platform 8 in Kings Cross railway station.

Ginghams' is pleasant enough but it's Basil that makes me go 'WOW!'

Basil doesn't just clear tables. He works like a man possessed.

Basil doesn't walk, he flies, running from table to table, cleaning, polishing, and clearing plates.

With all the skill of a world champion juggler he moves cups and trays and plates and ashtrays. Every last detail is a polished part of his performance.

And just as you think he has finished, two foil ashtrays leap from a top pocket and land right on target.

Basil doesn't clear tables.

Basil performs.

Basil entertains.

Basil is a star.

And he still has time for the customer, a cheeky greeting, a risqué joke. It's all just part of the show and the customers love it. Those that are there for the first time look blankly at each other and then join in with the laugh. So contagious is Basil's performance that I now allow extra time on my journey just so that I can visit Gingham's.

I tell this story in the hope that it inspires you to do something special. Whatever you do, do it with passion, do it with flair and panache.

My very special thanks to Basil for inspiring me.

Footnote: Gingham's Restaurant is no longer a feature of King's Cross Station. But I know that wherever Basil is, he will be delighting his customers.

School Dinners

When Louise Straughn decided to return to work, after the birth of her second daughter, she decided that she needed a job that enabled her to be at home during the school holidays and hit upon the idea of being a school dinner lady. Perfect for the holidays and easy enough to get into, even if she does not fit the stereotype of school dinner ladies from many of our childhood memories.

In my day they were all large, scowling women, wrapped in green overalls, defying you not to eat their lumpy mash, runny greens and cardboard, tasteless meat. By contrast, Louise is a smiling bubbly blonde who would be a good advertisement for her own cooking.

She started at a first school and over the years ran the kitchens in a number of schools, each time moving up the age range and taking on bigger schools. Whether catering for 50 infants or over 600 students and teachers, right from the start Louise tackled the role with a sense of enthusiasm and fun. Always introducing new ideas and going beyond the confines of her job description, she rewrote the definition of what a dinner lady in an educational establishment could achieve. Today she works at County Hall in Northumberland, where she passes on her experience and ideas to all the county's 200 plus educational and day centre catering establishments.

One of her first initiatives was to start a luncheon club for senior citizens, thus linking the young and old through her culinary and social skills. She was able to do this at low and therefore affordable costs merely by ordering more of the basic meat and two veg ingredients. This proved so popular that within weeks of introducing the service the demand from the older people was such that it became a twice-weekly event. This initiative led to many alliances between young and old and has been repeated, with great success at every school at which she worked.

Her next innovation was to start a breakfast club. As a mum herself, she reasoned that she would never send her children out in the morning without a good breakfast inside them but she noticed that for many of the kids, the lunch she provided was their first meal of the day.

For a modest charge she provided toast and cereal from 7.45 am onwards and for many pupils she was able to improve the quality of their daily lives and this was reflected in better schoolwork and improved behaviour in class.

Throughout her career working in schools, Louise has never lost sight of the many sets of customers that she serves:

Pupils
Teachers and Governors
Parents
Educational Authority
Catering colleagues / staff
Local community

As she started to work in schools with older pupils, Louise was able to involve them in the design of menus and discussions about healthy eating. Without making it a big authoritative issue, she was able to instigate debates and let the students decide menus with the art classes actually producing them.

Another of her initiatives – 'take five'- was designed to encourage students to maintain their recommended five portions of fruit and vegetables a day. She merely laid out a wide selection of fruit and vegetables each day so that students could just try one or two that perhaps they had not tasted before, without committing to a full portion.

Having gained the trust and respect of the students, Louise found that many would confide in her and she was able to help them with help on dieting when overweight, skin blemishes and the role of healthy eating and to steer them away from anorexia.

One of her messages was that skipping meals and crash diets were not the answer to weight loss ambitions. For girls of young teenage years, wanting to look slim and not have spots is often associated with the discovery of their sexuality and sometimes the pupils wanted to discuss matters outside the issues of food. She discovered that many girls went to her rather than their own mums but she was careful to preserve the balance between confidentiality and parental rights.

On one occasion, Louise was able to play a pivotal role, together with the parents and health professionals in assisting a pupil well on the way to serious anorexia problems.

Never forgetting the fun side of her job, Louise became legendary in her schools for her theme days. Whenever she could she would arrange a theme and produce special menus to reflect the theme. Whether it was a Chinese, Italian, Greek, US Independence Day,

Halloween, Valentines Day, Diwali or Medieval, Louise and her team would provide food for the occasion and dress in costume for the event. Even many of the teachers would join in the fun and dress accordingly, especially if the subject matter reflected their curriculum.

Becoming a school governor herself provided Louise with a further insight into the importance of integrating the kitchen with the aims of the school as a whole and not just being an ancillary department that produced the obligatory lunchtime meal.

She took on wider duties including cooking a grand dinner for several hundred at the school's 25th anniversary and involving herself and the school in the community's Healthy Heart Day, designed to encourage the adult population to eat more healthily.

She also won the North East's Chef of the Year for educational and local authority catering and represented the region in the national finals. She was a finalist and special award winner in the first ever National Customer Service Awards and as a result became something of a local personality, being invited by the Rotary Club to visit Arizona for a ten-day tour to represent the region on a goodwill visit.

At every twist and turn of her career, Louise has striven to be innovative in providing the very best service that she can. She has never rested on her laurels or been content to do merely what was asked of her. The best example of her determination to provide the best possible service in whatever conditions prevail occurred when the roof fell in on her kitchen one year just before Christmas.

It happened one morning when she and her team were about to start preparations for the day's lunch. Suddenly the roof started to creek and then large cracks appeared. Realising the danger, she rapidly evacuated her staff from the building and soon afterwards the roof caved in on the kitchen without anyone being hurt.

The rest of the school, housed in the main building were unaffected, except for the fact that it did not look like anyone was getting lunch that day. Louise however is made of sterner stuff. After having made sure that she had correctly reported the incident to the authorities and that they had taken over responsibility for the building, she and her team jumped into their cars and bought up just about every loaf of bread, roll and sandwich filling they could find in the nearby small town.

They then returned to the dining hall, set up a production line filling sandwiches and preparing quick soup; just finishing in time to serve the whole school with a lunch as usual. Well, not quite as usual but everyone got fed and some pupils enjoyed it so much that they asked for sandwiches and soup to be a regular meal.

Even then Louise was not finished. The kitchen would need to be restored over the forthcoming Christmas holidays but for the remainder of the term the kitchen would be out of action and that would mean that there would be no school dinners.

Once again, Louise rose to the occasion. She arranged for herself and her team to borrow the kitchen in a relatively nearby school. She and her team got in early, before their school cooks needed the facility, cooked the meal for the school then drove it down in relays to their own dining room. It meant some compromises in menu selection and a lot of extra work but everyone had a meal every day that term when it would have been easier and perfectly acceptable for Louise to have accepted the offer to suspend service.

Louise Straughn is a real customer service champion when it comes to providing great service and going that extra mile, all the time.

Looking After Dad –
Sian Robinson at Marriott Hotel, Swansea

Angie Court has been a follower of The WOW! Awards from the very early days. And as Director of Customer Service at Avis Europe PLC, Angie is always on the lookout for exceptional service. So I was delighted when she wrote to me about Sian Robinson:

> "Here is my nomination for a special lady who delivers exceptional customer service every time I visit her hotel. Her name is Sian Robinson. She works in the restaurant of the Swansea Marriott hotel.
>
> I take my elderly (very wobbly, wrinkly and deaf) father down there to visit my mother's grave (she was Welsh) every 3 months or so. Sian has gone out of her way to make him feel welcome and special.
>
> This last weekend they had severe staff shortages and Sian was working back to back shifts over several days - getting very little time to sleep and recover. I could see the strain and the tired lines, because I knew - but the other customers wouldn't have noticed any difference.
>
> Her manner with all the customers was continually friendly and warm. But with my father she still went overboard with him and every morning and evening made a huge fuss over him. He came away feeling 20 years younger because of the extra attention and her attention to detail.
>
> Sian always wows us so I am used to her - but this time she drew on all her spare energy to make a special show."

What a fantastic nomination!

And when I called Swansea Marriott to tell them about the nomination, they offered to have Angie stay as their guest when she went to present The WOW! Award.

Fantastic!

Not Quite Florence – Julie Nightingale, Marks & Spencer

This story was not a nomination for The WOW! Awards. It appeared in the national papers and is so amazing that I wanted to share it with you too.

Pensioner Annie Bates regularly has breakfast at her local Marks & Spencer store.

In fact, she has been having breakfast there every morning for the past two years. And, despite being 96 years old, she walks the 3 mile round trip for her toasted teacake and a cup of fresh coffee every morning.

But waitress Julie Nightingale was worried and knew that something was wrong when Annie failed to turn up for two days running.

Julie rushed to Annie's house where she found Annie collapsed on the floor. Annie had taken a fall and had been lying on the floor for quite a while. She could not stand up and she didn't have a phone.

Thanks to Julie's prompt action Annie was taken to hospital where she received treatment for her injuries.

Sometimes people ask me what lengths they should go to, to look after their customers. If everyone were to leave their place of work to go and check on the customer then surely the business is going to suffer.

My answer to this is that you have to do what you believe is right. Sometimes customer service goes beyond all the normal business boundaries. After all, we are only human.

Dan the Man – Dan Lewis, Orange Retail

Dan Lewis a phone 'Trainer' of Orange Retail has been nominated by Jon Morter.

"Dan, a phone 'trainer' as they're known, was superb.

The store is tiny yet at the time was packed with customers, yet Dan was patient with me in dealing with my relative ignorance on the new gadget style phones available. All good and bad points on each phone were briefed precisely, and I was not rushed or pushed into making a decision.

Once I'd made the decision he sorted the relevant paperwork out very quickly remembering that at the very beginning of the sale I'd said that I was on a lunch break...

Then there was a problem...when processing the form Dan was told over the phone that a new handset couldn't be given to me because my tariff was not paid up to date by a week or so. I hadn't realized this so I apologized to Dan for wasting his time at a busy period like this, and said I'd get back to him the following day after settling my account.

Dan was fantastic. He reserved the phone with my name on and said he would sort out the odds and ends for me before I returned.

As my lunch break was finishing fast I left the store. Before I even reached work (5 minutes) I received a call from Dan on my (old) mobile...he had spoken to Orange in my absence and managed to sort it out for today if I can return to the store...WOW!

The unfortunate thing was that there was no way I could really return to the store that day as there was loads of work for me to catch up on. Dan then said that he'd walk over to where I worked later in the evening once he had finished work (this is not exactly an easy walk...especially on a cold December evening!).

Later on at about 8:30pm...Dan turned up with a bag containing my new phone and the paperwork. The paperwork was already handwritten out with my details so all I had to do was sign the dotted line...WOW!

...and all this was a couple of days before Christmas, when most workers just want to get home ASAP after they finish...

Just to top it off, I went in to Orange yesterday to buy a car adaptor for it and Dan remembered my name and asked how the phone was for me."

I cannot imagine Jon ever thinking about going to any phone store other than Orange Retail in future.

Vision

Progress and development would be in small incremental steps if it were not for the vision of a few.

To be able to consider what might be possible and then communicate that to a group of people in such a way that they share the dream, is a true gift.

No matter how big or small the business, if it is given a vision that is vibrant and colourful, that people can support, then that business can achieve what others might consider impossible.

Mid Kent College – Frontliners: training with real customer service experience

With its closeness to the continent, there has always been a feeling of travel and adventure in the Kentish air and in recent years, with the opening of the Channel tunnel and many travel and tourism operations based in the area; that feeling has increased.

The travel, tourism and leisure industries hold out the promise of exciting careers for many of the area's young people seeking an interesting role in an industry offering travel and variety compared to the office or shelf-filling jobs that are the more normal offerings available to many.

The problem is that many school leavers with the desire to enter these roles, with a high customer contact element, have neither the educational or social skills demanded by prospective employers. As a result many youngsters, with potential, were denied the opportunity of pursuing their dreams.

Enter Christina Wells an energetic and innovative member of the Mid Kent College, who developed the idea of a customer service training course, with practical and relevant work experience, leading to an NVQ qualification and, more importantly an increased chance of a career in ones chosen field.

She looked hard at the situation and devised the country's first-ever college NVQ course in customer service. Initially this was designed as a two-year course and included all elements of customer service. NVQs are, of course, qualifications based on work based assessment and the confines of an academic institution do not ordinarily offer the opportunity for such assessment.

After much consideration the "Frontliners" were born. This was an innovative scheme that would combine classroom, theoretical training with actual assignments on behalf of genuine customers who would hire the young men and women, who comprised the Frontliners, to provide frontline services at various events requiring their services.

This was a bold move by the college, who needed to invest not only in tutors and classrooms but also in uniforms and marketing. Before the team could be offered to anyone, some basic training and ground rules had to be established. Travel and tourism might sound like glamorous roles to young impressionable people but the reality can often involve the discipline needed to perform some routine, not to say tedious and repetitive tasks.

One of the first steps was to design a suitable uniform to be worn when working on an event that would identify the team members. It had to be smart and project a good image whilst, at the same time, being practical. The eventual design was based on aircrew uniform, complete with hat and gloves (optional at customer's choice). When working on an event the Frontliners always wear the full uniform as specified or a uniform provided by the customer, for example, special T-shirt when working at a rock concert.

The first thing the students needed to learn was that when in uniform, they become customer service and event management professionals. Like all event managers, they soon get to realise that, no matter how well planned an event may be, sometimes things can and will go wrong. In that situation, the Frontliners are taught that there is no room for recriminations, as the objective remains to make the event work. Although they may not be major decision makers or senior members of the event organisation, they are trained never to make a negative comment about the event that they are involved with, whether it is about the weather, the delegates or the event management.

The range of events that the Frontliners have worked on since their formation is both wide and varied. From hosting VIP guests at their local football team, Gillingham FC, Elton John rock concerts and the BBC Good Food Guide at the NEC Birmingham through to being invited to work at the National Customer Service Awards at the Grosvenor House Hotel after winning the Innovation category the previous year. They have gone on to work at several other events organised by Quest Media, the promoters of the National Customer Service Awards, including sister award programmes, National Business Awards, National Sales Awards and British Computer Society Awards and conferences including Best Practice in Customer Service and the Institute of Customer Service Annual Conference. They have also worked at the Society of Consumer Affairs Professionals' Annual Conference.

With such an impressive list of events, providing great experience for the students, it is not surprising that they gain a great insight into customer service and dealing with all kinds of customers and their demands. It is not surprising that such experience builds both a skill set for the student to offer to potential employers and a fantastic C.V. to support job applications.

The Frontliners themselves come from a variety of backgrounds. The area covered by Mid-Kent College includes a diversity of socio-economic and cultural influences and all are represented by the mix of students. For the most part they are youngsters just out of 5th form with a modest collection of academic qualifications. Despite their different backgrounds they quickly blend as a team, united by a common purpose. The course is not restricted to school leavers and several mature students have taken their place amongst the ranks of the Frontliners and have seen their careers transformed as a result.

Clearly the two-year course covers classroom learning as well as the on-the-job work experience and the students work towards an NVQ qualification. The course work includes a wide range of theory relating to how to handle customers and their likely responses and this is then tested in practice when working on assignments.

The most important factor in assessing the success of the Frontliners is to examine what happens to them when completing the course.

The majority quickly finds work in frontline customer service roles and, indeed, several have made it to air crew positions. There are even examples of some of the earlier students returning to college to lead the programme.

Again it is necessary to examine what lessons can be gleaned from this case study, because most readers will be working for a single organisation and not a college with an ongoing throughput of trainees.

1. Again we are looking at the results of creative thinking. Until Christine launched this scheme there was not a single college course open for specific customer service training despite the size of the market and demand for people with the right skills.

2. The standards that were applied were carefully thought through as being relevant for the role and rigorously maintained, because they were right for the role or, to quote from today's business jargon 'fit for purpose'.

3. The Frontliners live their course. When they have completed their training and find themselves dealing with customers, they only have to learn about the products and processes of their employer, because the habits and skills involved in helping customers are universal and by the time these guys are employed they are second nature.

Where Does the Pilot Stay?
The Arora International Hotel, Heathrow

John Shackleton nominated this hotel after getting fabulous service when he was running a training day there. The overall experience was great and one individual in particular gave John a WOW! moment. Here's what John told me.

"I was running a training day for a client recently at the Arora International Hotel, Gatwick and as I'd never been before I arrived very early (8:00 am).

I was met as I came through the door by a smiling young man, Vincent Madden, who asked me what I was there for and could he help me. After I had explained he led me to my training room checked all the equipment etc and introduced me to the staff that would be helping me that day.

We had a great day's training, everything in place when we asked for it, great food at lunchtime and wonderful service from all the staff, all day.

At 5:00 p.m. I was leaving and I spotted Vincent in his usual place near the front door. I congratulated him on his own actions and said how impressed I had been with the general level of customer service in the hotel, especially the staff's attention to detail. He thanked me for my feedback and gave me his card.

He turned out to be no less than the DIRECTOR OF OPERATIONS for the hotel and had spent all day greeting guests and showing an excellent example to all his staff of top class customer service."

As I write this report, I'm actually sitting in the lounge area of The Arora International. It's 8.50 a.m. and I'm here for the presentation of The WOW! Award at 10.00 a.m.

It's good to be here early. It gives me a chance to take a look at the hotel for myself. Do they really deserve The WOW! Award. Here's what I've experienced so far:-

I phoned the hotel from a car park a few miles away and asked if someone could give me directions. The young man who answered my call was extremely helpful.

What I particularly liked was that he reassured me that I was very close and then gave me directions that included lots of landmarks. You know how it is when you're in a strange area. Road names are often difficult to spot but a police station, a college and a railway bridge were very easy.

I'm not sure where best to leave my car so I ask at reception. The young lady suggests a closer and safer parking space for me within the hotel car park. "Simply take a ticket from the machine and the parking is free."

There is an extremely comfortable lounge, friendly courteous service and an air of calm prevails. I feel very relaxed sitting here. Maybe it's the gentle sound from the spectacular waterfall that soothes my nerves after my long car journey.

I start to look at the other guests. This hotel is very close to Gatwick and I'm not surprised to see that a lot of aircrew are staying here. It's noticeable that they seem to be enjoying themselves here. Given that they must stay in a lot of hotels around the world, this strikes me as a good sign.

Hmmm. I think that I would like to be a guest here.

Come 9.45 and it's time to meet the General Manager John Donaldson. John is very interested in my first impressions and I'm extremely interested in what they do.

It turns out that The Arora concept started at Heathrow and was a complete turn around on the normal basis for running hotels. Instead of aiming at the general public, they built a hotel to accommodate aircrew from British Airways.

They started with the idea of trying to offer a better value proposition than other hotels. For instance, all pricing points reflect normal retail prices. So if you buy a drink in the bar you pay the same as you would in the pub down the road. And telephone calls are charged at normal call rates rather than the excessive rates that are common to so many hotels.

Consequently John tells me, "We're winning business instead of stealing it! But it's all about service levels and exceeding customer expectations."

Nice approach, John.

John goes on to explain, "We recruit for personality predominantly – the right appearance and the right personality traits. You can graft on the technical knowledge. And we do a huge amount of training.

We use situation analysis training. We take a 'camera-shot' of where I am now and 'how can I deal with this situation in a non-prescriptive way?' We find that people who don't have the right personality traits cannot handle this very well.

Recently, I had heard the story of a customer who was refused entry to a cinema because they had purchased an ice cream from another store. I asked John how he would react if I were to come into the hotel lounge with a drink or an ice cream from another store. 'No problem,' he replied. "'If a customer came into our lounge drinking a product that was purchased from a local store, I'd have no problem with that.'

Hmmm. Nice approach.

No wonder all the aircrew here look so happy.

I didn't know that I needed it – but I Want One of Those!

In May 2006, internet gift shop "I Want One of Those" (or IWOOT for short) started telling their customers about The WOW! Awards. In the next 12 months we received over 1000 nominations from delighted customers.

These are just a few of those nominations – just the way that we received them in the customers' own words.

Alex Clay said:

> "Every time I have ordered from IWOOT it has been with a rather large sense of urgency.
>
> Each and every time it has felt like IWOOT do everything in their power to ensure I get my order in time for the event in question. Once they even organized a courier so I could get my gift within a few hours!
>
> This time I needed some gifts for Mothers' Day, but was unable to complete the transaction online. Sally was more than helpful ensuring I was able to receive the order the next day. Without her assistance, my life would not have been worth living, for the next week or so at least!"

Angela Riches told us:

> "I came across this site purely by chance as I was browsing for gifts. It made me laugh so much. I am suffering from cancer so anything that cheers me up deserves an award in my books.

They sell some clever and fairly sensible gifts and gadgets as well as some really amusing very good value things which, when I received my order, made me want to keep them for myself rather than give away as intended. Therefore I will very soon place another order with them.

I only had needed to contact them as I placed my order on line, to verify they had received the small questionnaire which followed the order form. I accidentally submitted it as my mouse skid out of control. Hence they replied and a couple of helpful messages passed back and forth.

Matt was the man who answered my email re the questionnaire. Their descriptions on site of the goods they sell are in themselves a source of hilarity and true to form which I can say from experience.

My specialist at the Royal Marsden I know will adore his skeleton mouse mat which I ordered from IWOOT. I think I spent at least two hours looking at everything on the site. It makes life for people like me who are in constant pain and often housebound for long periods, a very much happier patient.

I hope they win an award. They deserve one for bringing laughter to people especially people such as myself who cannot access many sources of entertainment. They are a curious, comical, competitive, compulsive and caring bunch of people who know that what the world really needs is more fun and laughter.

I love them."

Annie Smith reported:

"Through my own foolishness I didn't read the small print on my order details and ended up not having my order dispatched, possibly ruining Jean's birthday party in the process!!

I used the online 'Live Help' facility to speak to Sally at IWOOT who sorted it all out for me. It is an excellent alternative to sitting on hold for what can seem like an eternity trying to get through to a call centre.

An immediate dispatch was arranged on a courier, which Sally organized with speed, maintaining constant contact and demonstrating excellent customer care skills. I feel that this company (and individual) was working hard to show that I am valued as a customer.

Makes a refreshing change!"

Ben Legg said:

"Customer service isn't about a one off experience.

Every time I order from IWOOT the order is handled quickly and efficiently, and the one time I did have a problem with an order they sorted it out very quickly and courteously.

I know I can trust them and that's what good customer service is about."

Heather Holland told us:

"Whenever I've ordered from iwantoneofthose.com their efficiency, courtesy, professionalism and prompt service is second to none.

I was particularly impressed on my birthday a couple of weeks ago when they sent me a 'happy birthday' email and a £5 discount towards my next order."

I Want One of Those was selected as a finalist for the 2006 National Customer Service Awards. And as a result, I was able to find out a little bit more about the company and how it is organized.

When the company was started in June 2000 their mission was simply "to WOW! customers." And they have always tried to be fun, honest and entertaining in the way that they do business. For instance, if a telephone caller has to be put on hold they will be entertained with a series of mini James Bond adventures. And, as a result, the callers often ask to be put back on hold!

One of their objectives has been to promote themselves through word of mouth and to maintain customer loyalty. And as a result approximately one third of their new customers come from word-of-mouth referrals.

They also go to great lengths to make a customer feel valued and aim to answer telephone calls in less than 10 seconds. In fact, with the exception of the Xmas period, calls are usually answered in less than six seconds!

But it's not just their use of the telephone that makes their communication special. From the moment that an online customer adds something to their shopping basket they have the option to engage in a live chat facility. And customers receive a series of emails which include an acknowledgement, an order confirmation and a dispatch email.

When it comes to recruitment, the number one aim is to find people who have the right personality and fit into the culture of the business. Customer Service staff are eligible for a bonus for every personal customer commendation. And there is presently a £100 bonus each month for the most outstanding team member. All employees are empowered to treat customers as individuals and to make decisions.

I Want One of Those consider that they are responsible for a customer's order until the goods are actually received and accepted by the customer. This is not about a one-off experience; the service delivery has to be consistent. Weekly team meetings and monthly meetings with the managing director all help to focus the team and enhance the customer experience.

Their commitment to making deliveries on time is extraordinary. All orders received by 3 p.m. are dispatched the same day under their standard delivery option. They even offer a same day delivery service for the London area. They have regular meetings with Parceline to review their performance and work together on maintaining this high standard.

Through working hard on customer service they have also been able to grow their sales. One of the things that they realised was that it is often helpful for a customer to be able to chat online with one of their representatives. And so, each representative may now be involved in up to six online live chats with customers. This is provided at no charge to the customer and as well as enhancing the service has helped to reduce the number of dropouts in the ordering process.

Trying to be as honest as they possibly can with their customers is well reflected in their website.

The founder of I Want One of Those set out to change the face of retail but realised it was not about selling products. It's much more about having fun!

I Want One of Those has already grown to more than £10 million in annual sales. And they feel that they are still at the beginning of their journey.

I Want One of Those were recognised for their achievements and declared the overall winner of The WOW! Awards in 2006.

Universal Soldiers

One of the challenges facing organisations trying to give great customer service is that the resources can be stretched during peak periods and at these times, despite the best efforts of the organisation's customer service professionals, delays can occur and mistakes can creep in. Additionally, with all the goodwill in the world, staff can be tempted to adopt a 'Well what do you expect? I am doing my best,' attitude.

Shops at Christmas and at sales time are prime examples. Annual billing time for certain kinds of business and bank holidays for the leisure industry are further examples.

Financial services is another industry where deadlines and trigger dates can lead to bottle necks and other self-imposed deadlines relating to special promotions can bring about a similar situation. Other occurrences that can lead to a temporary fall in standards arise from staff shortages brought about by a spate of maternity absences or an unexpected build up of staff attrition.

All of the above can give rise to situations where temporarily normal standards fall away and often this is the very time when customers are looking for reassurance from the organisation with which they have entrusted their savings, investments or pensions.

AXA Life found a successful solution to this problem a few years ago when they formed a special team of versatile individuals known as

"Universal Soldiers". This team has multi-skilled individuals who, whilst identifying with the Universal Soldiers team, can be parachuted into various departments – either individually or in small teams – to help out in any department where their skills are needed.

Although it takes a special kind of person to be a Soldier - they have to be high achievers and role models for other staff - there are no shortage of volunteers for the team. The variety of work and the opportunity to try new departments are attractive to many of the company's customer service professionals keen to build their careers and CVs with the widest range of experiences possible.

The end of the tax year is an obvious demand for the Soldiers but in financial services there are frequently special situations where suddenly a particular department falls under pressure.

The Soldiers have to be able to work as part of the team that they are helping at any time but at the same time retain their Universal Soldier identity. They will continue to meet with other Soldiers through team meetings and team building sessions. They work both in back office and contact centre environments and during quieter times may be sent into a department just for experience so that they have the appropriate knowledge when the real call comes.

At AXA Life, the Soldiers have helped to build a lean operation able to meet high service standards, whilst helping to reduce costs. Many of the team are Six Sigma trained, gaining their belts whilst helping the company improve quality standards whilst driving costs down by 10% per year.

One of the downside of the skills and excellence of the Soldiers and their reputation is that many of them are coveted by the various departments who frequently request that the person concerned is assigned to them permanently. Quite often the suggested appointment involves a promotion for the Soldier concerned and when there is a fit between the requirements of the requesting department and the aspirations of the Soldier, the transfer makes sense for the company.

So successful are the Soldiers and such is their reputation that every few years the whole team is replenished as the established members take up permanent roles and new Soldiers are recruited. However with plenty of volunteers ready to step in and with the old Soldiers acting as ambassadors for the project in their new roles the future of the Soldiers is bright and should continue for as long as variety, challenge and deadlines remain a part of the highly important and technical financial services business. On that basis the Soldiers will be a regular part of the delivery of great service at AXA Life for many years to come.

Jaine Lays Down the Law! – The Gourmet Sandwich Company

Philip Turner nominated owner Jaine Ellison after seeing a poster in her shop at Otley. This is what it said on the poster:

As some of you may already be aware, I am the new owner of this wonderful establishment.

I'd like to take this opportunity to tell you a little about myself, confessions first.

I have never done anything like this before! For my sins, I have spent the last 16 years employed as a defendant personal injury lawyer in Leeds City Centre.

One day, I'd decided I'd had enough. I couldn't face one more day arguing why it was unreasonable to claim Mrs. Bloggs could never work again after stubbing her big toe! I wanted out, so here I am – how's that for an honest lawyer!

Just to confuse you, I am also a bodybuilder! Indeed I am the A.N.B. British Champion for the second year running (and 4th in the world!) – you may have seen me in the local papers (looking much trimmer than at present!!). I'll be attempting to defend my title at the end of the year!

I intend putting my knowledge on diet and nutrition to good use. I will gradually introduce a new range of 'healthy' options – don't panic, this is in addition to the existing menu – I'm also partial to the odd big breakfast too!

Feel free to ask me any diet-related questions, and I will do my best to help you. If you have any particular requests now's the time to grab me and let me know…

Thanks for reading this – just one more thing, should I have a relapse and charge you £180.00 for your lunch one day just remind me I'm no longer a lawyer and to get in the real world!!!

Cheers,

Jaine xx   ☺

WOW!

We all want to fall in love with our suppliers? You just can't help falling in love with Jaine the minute you read her poster.

It's an inspired piece of writing. Jaine has revealed her weaknesses and her commitment to help. Can you ever imagine going into The Gourmet Sandwich Company and not getting great service?

What commitment have you made to your customers?

When I'm working with businesses around the world helping them to improve their customer service, I often show them this poster. It's great to see the Chief Executives of some very large companies thinking very hard about how they can match a poster from The Gourmet Sandwich Shop in Otley.

ECourier – New kids on the block

This case study from the National Customer Service Awards looks to the future and features a small company that has launched recently with great success, focusing heavily on customer needs.

By breaking the mould of inter-city courier companies eCourier launched in 2004 have carved a niche for themselves as one of London's most successful courier companies and indeed are one of the fastest growing logistics firms in Europe.

Their story is exciting for its own reasons: the main players are young, enthusiastic entrepreneurs with a strong international flavour. They combine street-smart savvy with strong academic and I.T. skills. This is a story of a business start-up and the success is due much to the energy and enterprise of its charismatic founders but it was the customer vision that won them an award in the National Customer Service Awards 2005.

The principals of the company – Tom Allason, a young ambitious Englishman and Jay Bregman, a charismatic American met whilst studying at Dartmouth College in the US. Tom returned to England to work for a shipping company in London and Jay also came to the UK to do a graduate course at the London School of Economics. They were later joined by the young German academic Dr Christian Ahlert who had been making a name for himself in cutting edge research at the Oxford Internet Institute where he had previously worked with Bregman.

The company was borne out of the frustration that Tom experienced with the levels of service available in the same day courier market in his role as a shipping broker. Particularly he was unnerved that anytime he called with a query on a booking for a delivery crossing the city, he was unable to obtain any response other than 'he is five minutes away' which strained credulity in the not uncommon situation which saw him still waiting thirty minutes later. He believed that there had to be a better way to provide customer-focused courier services.

After six months or so of preliminary research they formed the company in September 2003 but the planning and preparation was still in the early stage and it was to be another twelve months before the first delivery was executed. Their initial view of the market revealed the courier industry was in a sad state. Years of relentless competition amongst numerous providers all selling precisely the same inconsistent service with no added value, combined with a low barrier to entry, has commoditised the courier market leading to single digit margins and a perception amongst customers that price was the only differentiator between courier service providers. Most significantly, this environment had created a general malaise among operators and customers that things would not change. This was a service industry in which the customer was not king.

The industry had gone largely untouched by the information revolution that had been affecting virtually every other sector of British business. Even more unusual in the modern day was that this backwardness had led to conventional courier operators suffering diseconomies of scale. Tom and Jay believed deeply that technology could be used not only to re-engineer the conventional market dynamics and provide value-added offerings but also that superior customer service itself, independent of any technological bells and whistles, could act as a competitive advantage. The typical industry view, by comparison, was that customer service was useful only in crisis management – when deliveries went horribly wrong, customer service helped prevent accounts being closed.

In traditional courier firms, lack of technological sophistication is a barrier to meeting customer expectations. Customers use couriers for mission-critical deliveries with very tight time windows. They often require proof of delivery and real time status updates. However, in traditional firms, proof of delivery information is recorded manually on paper sheets carried by couriers and, if clients request it, they have to wait until the courier returns to his office at the end of the week to turn in his sheets to the company. Status information is not available because control has no way of proactively monitoring where couriers are at any time without calling out over the radio and, if they are able to raise the courier, trusting his or her response. In short, customers demand a level of information and control about their deliveries which traditional operators are unable to provide.

eCourier wanted to build an infrastructure whereby individual clients would be given the same or better levels of information about their packages – in real time – as was available to the company and the courier. All couriers would carry handheld computers linked to Global Positioning System satellites to pinpoint location to 10 metre accuracy. Signatures would be collected on touch screens and uploaded instantly to eCourier's web site. Further, a street level tracking facility would enable customers to follow their couriers traversing the streets of the UK to their delivery points. Finally, a live chat facility would capitalise on the popularity of instant messaging systems to replace the burden of phone calls to make amendments or for additional enquiries. Taken together, the implementation of those innovations provides customers with exceptional control of their courier deliveries.

One further problem existed – service. In traditional operations deliveries are allocated to couriers via radio by human controllers. This is an error-prone process which places natural limits on the scale of any one company. The costs of employing banks of human controllers also erode margins to the point where the courier salaries had remained stagnant over the last decade - a period which had seen staggering increases in the cost of being a courier due to, *inter alia*, higher fuel prices and rising insurance premiums. This meant that many companies had resorted to hiring less qualified and less knowledgeable couriers. By creating a system whereby incoming bookings are automatically dispatched to the couriers without human intervention, Tom and Jay reasoned, they could not only make their company scalable and more profitable but also use the increased margins to hire the most professional couriers and thereby improve service times and, consequently customer satisfaction.

They decided initially to concentrate purely on the same day delivery market within London. In itself this is a big market worth an estimated £425m per annum and consisting of over 10,000 freelance couriers. However it is also an extremely fragmented market with over 600 operators, the largest of which commands 3.5% of market share.

They tapped into their academic contacts and sought the best business planning and technology help they could draw upon. Jay used his last days at LSE to scour the library for peer-reviewed research which might indicate academics qualified to build the Advanced Information Based Allocation (AIBA) system – which became their codename for the courier automatic allocation system. Jay obtained a list of top researchers in relevant fields and distributed to them a comprehensive request for a proposal document that specified in great detail the nature of the problem that the automatic allocation system would need to solve.

This document was then distributed – on hastily designed eCourier letterhead and with budget business cards – to the academics. They were amazed at the response they got to their request and in particular they received tremendous assistance from the Massachusetts Institute of Technology in USA and the UNICAL & UNILE High Performance Computing Centres in Italy.

The philosophy behind the system design was to build an IT infrastructure where everyone, including the customer, knew where all the couriers were and what they were doing at all times. Developed with the help of leading minds and research laboratories in logistics and computing, the system can then predict times for all deliveries and can automatically intervene to allocate the most appropriate courier for a new delivery. The details are automatically routed to that courier, via his mobile computer and he just imputs to confirm that the job is noted and accepted. No other human intervention is necessary in the allocation of new orders.

As a result they have been able to reduce the banks of human controllers thereby improving operating margins, whilst simultaneously improving accuracy of resource allocation and with it the gross margin. As a matter of interest the team claim that the same-day courier business has a kind of contra "economy of scale" rule in that the more couriers there are the more controllers you need, the errors and confusion increase and extra cost is incurred in further layers of controllers and compensation for errors. For eCourier, costs are much reduced and some of this can be returned to the business in terms of keen pricing and better pay for the couriers and, of course, investment in real customer service.

When a delivery is made, the system sends back to the sender a proof of delivery email containing the recipient's digital signature within ten seconds of signing. This is another area of increased customer satisfaction as once the package is known to be delivered the customer's concerns are at an end.

All of this enables the company to provide a superior, cost efficient service that allows them to compete on price, without sacrificing profitability, with even the largest courier providers. Furthermore customers have online, accurate and continually updated information on both pick-up and delivery times. The couriers carry hand held computers that, despite the complexity of the underlying technicalities are easy to use and far more efficient than the mobile phone systems primarily used by rivals.

From the customers' point of view, they can access the website, obtain a quotation for their order and then, having placed the order online, track its progress throughout and know the instant that delivery has been affected. If necessary a distribution manager can keep track of multiple deliveries, with various destinations, all at the same time.

The tracking system is superimposed on a street level map and the customer can literally track any, or all of their bookings at once, as the couriers navigate their way through the streets of London. Rather than providing a rough update of courier positions, eCourier provide supreme accuracy by offering customers the same mapping technology as their own staff in the control centre.

So far we have mainly examined the customer service benefits arising from technology and it was primarily this that won them the E-Commerce Award in the 2005 National Customer Service Awards (and, incidentally, two Awards in the equally prestigious British Computer IT Professional Awards 2005). Technology alone will never result in outstanding customer service, however when looking at customer needs, technology can be used to find innovative ways to meet those needs. The company has also looked hard at the most important part of its customer experience....the couriers themselves.

Traditionally, couriers are poorly served by the courier companies who, in return, often receive less than professional standards from the couriers. The couriers, whether they are van drivers, cyclists or motor cyclists are vitally important to the companies as they are the face of the courier company to the customers and their performance and appearance represents the company in their eyes.

As already explained, during the last ten years or so, courier rates of pay remained flat as companies endeavoured to hold down prices to stay competitive. Courier costs have however risen tremendously in this time – fuel, insurance, vehicle maintenance, licences, protective clothing, congestion charges and general cost of living has all resulted in the courier's job becoming far less financially rewarding. As a result of this the number of truly professional couriers has reduced and there are many less professional operators in their place.

The company recognises the importance of their couriers and they have introduced a number of measures to attract and retain the best couriers. First of all they employ proper vetting procedures to ensure that their couriers are suitable for the role. They all have clean licences, no criminal records, properly serviced vehicles, all wear the company logo and know how to smile at customers and promote a positive image of the company.

Due to the cost efficiencies arising from the use of technology they are able to pay higher rates for the best couriers, most of whom come by way of recommendation from couriers already onboard. In fact, to cope with their fast expanding business demands, they have a waiting list of pre-qualified couriers.

Further courier benefits come in the provision of a facility at their main office, where couriers can meet, use the computer for their own purposes, eat and wash and freshen up. As a result the couriers are ambassadors for the business and frequently provide insights that lead to further business. It is also quite critical to recognise, as eCourier has, that their couriers perform an important customer interface for their own customers and are therefore ambassadors.

A still small, specialist courier company, working in a tight well defined market, with a bent on technology might not seem a company with a great message for customer service professionals reading this book. There are however many lessons that can be taken from this case study.

- Study your market. Think about what the weak points of service are. In many sectors a kind of status quo exists and it sometimes takes fresh eyes to see the weaknesses. Look at the business through the eyes of a customer as Tom did when working as a ship broker.

- Use research facilities available. These guys tapped into the academic avenues open to them. There is more research available to most of us, either free or at low cost, than we are often aware of. Check with trade and professional associations and local academic institutions. You are likely to be surprised at the help that is out there for you.

- Technology can provide fantastic customer solutions. Greater speed and reduced costs can often be achieved; providing you really know what the customer needs are.

- Do not rely on technology to deliver the service without the support of committed, enthusiastic staff who can manage the technology and relate personally and personably to customers.

- Do not get so carried away with technology that the role of key frontline staff is overlooked in the process. The role of the courier is vital in this business. The vehicles and the technology can be absolutely state of the art but it is the courier that the customer sees at the end of the process and the courier can cement the impression made by the efficiency of the process...or destroy it! The old adage "Happy staff, happy customers" remains true even in a world of technical perfection.

Absolute diamond - Gems TV

We received more than 36 nominations for Gems TV in just a few weeks during 2006. But this one really stood out for us.

Gillian Lucraft told us:

> "I've been looking for somewhere to nominate Gems TV for an award. Every time I've had a query, customer services have

been polite, listened to what I had to say and then got it sorted out immediately.

The entire company seems to be completely focussed on customer care, including the presenters, so much so that all of their email addresses are given out so that you can contact them direct.

Presenter Steve Ashton always replies to emails, sorts out special requests and having been told that I was going into hospital for an operation, took the time to enquire as to how I was and then sent me a copy of the Gems TV DVD.

In the world of shopping TV they stand head and shoulders above the rest and could teach many non TV companies a few things as well. These guys deserve an award."

The world is certainly changing and home shopping will continue to grow. It's great to know that the principles of customer service work just as well in this environment as they do for the more traditional channels.

Gems TV have adopted a "customers for life" approach. Their intention is that their customers proactively become their ambassadors. And that the customers are an extension of the family unit. In fact, many of their customer relationships are on a first name basis.

They always put principles before policy. Everyone is empowered to meet customer needs. And everyone is encouraged to use their initiative and be proactive. If they know that a customer likes a particular type of stone then they will let that customer know about new items before they are offered to the rest of their audience. They even offer a personal shopper service to find a specific item or pass a customer's specific request on to their design team in Thailand.

Their commitment to training certainly shows through in their service delivery. All of their people receive regular training and coaching in soft skills. Each team of 14 telephone operators has its own supervisor. And the supervisor will spend a minimum of 15 minutes each day with each operator as part of a coaching session. The sessions are to encourage good service and to encourage operators to feel good about what they are doing.

Many of the jewellery products and much of their customer service has been inspired by their customers. They use every possible means to encourage customer feedback including focus groups, response cards, e-mail, text messaging, outbound calls (especially to welcome customers back into the family) and customer visits.

This new forum for shopping has led to the development of technology tailored around the customer's needs. They have been so successful in this area that processing customer orders takes just 42 seconds on average.

In the last year they have had 248,000 customers. More than 24,000 customers completed one of their feedback forms and 98% of people would recommend Gems TV to a friend.

In their approach to customers they aim to entertain and educate, deliver fantastic quality and value, provide a VIP telephone experience, offer a no quibble money back guarantee, provide 'big picture outcome', aftercare service and a memorable shopping experience.

Gems TV want their business to be the best place that anyone has ever worked at. They use a combination of bonuses, spot price incentives and have an employee of the month award. It's all about having lots of fun!

Haringey – taking a lead in the public sector

Haringey Council is the first local authority to use The WOW! Awards.

The drive and determination to make this happen came from Chris McLean, Corporate Customer Focus Manager. Chris proposed that they run a pilot programme from June 2006 in just two departments - Registrars and Libraries and Arts and Museum services.

Chris called us just two days after the pilot started. She told us how excited they all were – 5 customer nominations had already been received!

One of the very first nominations was for the Alexandra Park Library. There is a weekly play and song group. This is what the customer told us:

> "It's a great place to meet other people. The singing is brilliant and the organiser has just a great personality that can pick up anyone on a rainy day. Please, you just have to be there in order to understand just how much fun it is. And you don't have to sing, but you will!"

In some cases, customers did not know the name of the person who served them. But it didn't stop them making a nomination. This customer told us:

> "I would like to nominate the young man who delivered the videos to me on the 15th.

He was 'hand-picked' for the job – courteous, pleasant, bright and respectful. He almost seemed too good for the job he was doing – as seen purely by me as recipient."

The customer told us about how she has returned to using the library at Muswell Hill:

"Some years ago I stopped using the library at Muswell Hill because I found the staff rude, indifferent and very unhelpful. It was very depressing!

I'm delighted to be back now enjoying my visits. All the staff members are courteous and extremely helpful, even when very busy. They even recognise me in the street!

How different from former times!"

Yet another nomination:

"I would never usually fill in a form like this, but the service I received yesterday was exceptional. The lady in question knew her job totally, she was very friendly and even though I was very nervous speaking to her, she put me at ease and went through the whole process with me.

I am recovering from a brain condition where I find it very difficult to converse with people, especially on the telephone. I wish all government and council departments had such friendly and efficient staff as yours.

This lady and the chap that called me back made what would normally be a traumatic experience for me a pleasant and easy transaction. Thank them both very much for me.

Congratulations on having such lovely warm and professional staff - a totally new and awesome experience!"

Following on from this successful pilot, Chris McLean prepared a report to recommend a way forward for Haringey Council. The following comments have been extracted from that report.

A pilot scheme was launched in the Registrar's and Libraries, Arts and Museum services in June 2006. **Its success has exceeded all expectations.**

The importance and significance of customer perceptions of Haringey's services together with the ease and attractiveness of opportunities for feedback are key concerns for the council. The WOW! Awards scheme could provide a further channel for such feedback. Its positive nature will help to further promote and reward the customer-focussed thinking and behaviour that is integral to delivering excellent services.

The overall success of the pilot has proved a positive experience all round. Customers have a new and quite different opportunity to give feedback on service received; staff feel better and more directly valued; remarkable front-line behaviour that would perhaps have not been brought to the attention of managers and the Heads of Service is now done so formally and last but not least, the scheme has provided very positive publicity for Haringey in both the local and trade press.

The success of the pilot has exceeded all expectations. Within the first 3 months 225 nominations were received - this compares with 147 compliments received for the entire council in 2005/6 under the existing compliments scheme. Nominations were attracted not only for the two services in the pilot but others as well, including two for contracted staff. These have been submitted by a wide range of customers too – including those whose first language is not English, children and businesses. It is clear that **the scheme has captured the public's imagination** and that **customers are increasingly sharing the council's confidence in front line services and the staff who deliver them.**

It is proposed that the WOW! Awards scheme be rolled out corporately and apply to all council services regardless of who they are delivered by – a matter largely irrelevant to our customers anyway.

The scheme should subsume the existing compliments provisions of the customer feedback scheme, so that any compliments received by any means are counted and included under the WOW! scheme.

The success of the pilot is a factor of its simplicity, ease of access and lack of bureaucracy and so we should look to run the corporate scheme along the same lines. The scheme should be publicised and enabled by putting posters up at all service delivery points (much as with publicity for the complaints scheme), along with leaflets and suggestion boxes. The posters and leaflets were designed for the pilot with a view to corporate applicability; apart from minor alterations, no work is required here. It makes sense for suggestion boxes to be corporately branded with a leaflet holder attached.

Public participation in the pilot has been used as evidence of the potential benefits to all stakeholders in rolling the WOW! Awards out corporately. Appropriate discussions have been held with the WOW! organisation, colleagues and input sought from staff in Central Feedback and Directorate complaints teams.

Rolling out the WOW! Awards scheme will bring benefits to all stakeholders – a means of **feedback to those who receive our services, personal recognition for those who deliver them well and aspiration for others** to do so. It should also help build on the council's improving reputation both locally, in the field of local government as well as within the customer service industry.

When The WOW! Awards were first launched I had a vision about how they might help businesses to improve their customer service by interacting with their customers. It's taken a long time and a lot of hard work. And I would like to make a special thank you to people like Chris McLean and businesses like Haringey Council for being the pioneers and helping to make it happen.

Exceeding Expectations – Surprise

The secret of great service is the ability to exceed customer's expectations.

Expectation minus 1 = failure! Expectation plus 1 = delight!

But our expectations are not just set by the business that we are dealing with at that moment. They are determined by every business that we have ever dealt with and in particular by those that we have dealt with most recently.

If you go out shopping and receive great service at the butchers then you may be disappointed when the greengrocer does not deliver at the same level. Or your expectation of phoning for help may depend on the last time that you got caught up in an automated answering system.

What really makes us go "WOW!" is when a business manages to delights us even when our expectations are at the highest level. It might not always be big things. In fact, it is often the little things that make the biggest differences in the eyes of a customer.

This section is devoted to the little surprises that make us say, "WOW! How did they think of that?"

The Richer Way – Richer Sounds

Richer Sounds first came to my attention in 1996 when a friend of a friend, Natalie Anderson, visited the Richer Sounds store in Leeds.

Natalie wanted to buy some audiocassettes. She found the ones that she wanted and took them to the counter to pay.

The sales assistant was very friendly and polite. He asked Natalie, 'What are you going to be recording?'

'Oh, just some bits of music. Nothing special,' replied Natalie.

The assistant took a different and more expensive pack of cassettes from the shelf. 'If you want to record music, I think you'll find these ones give you a much better quality.'

'Its okay,' said Natalie. 'The other ones will do fine.'

'Well try these and let me know what you think.' He popped the cassettes that Natalie had chosen and his recommended cassettes into a bag.

'I'm sorry!' exclaimed Natalie. 'But I haven't got enough money to buy both types.'

"That's okay. Just pay for the ones that you chose. Take these other cassettes as our gift and let me know how you get on."

Natalie was gob smacked. 'Why did you do that?' she asked.

'Because we're Richer Sounds,' came the reply.

Natalie had visited Richer Sounds in Leeds. Within 20 minutes of her visit, the story had been relayed to me in Stevenage.

Clearly there was something special going on at Richer Sounds and I was determined to find out more. It turns out that the business is run by Julian Richer. One of his shops had been in the Guinness Book of Records every year since 1991 for the highest retail sales per square foot of any shop in the world.

Richer Sounds has twice been voted the best British owned company to work for in the Sunday Times Best Company survey. And it has also been in the record books for the highest proportion of profits donated to charity.

Over the next few years our paths crossed many times. Julian and I both appeared as keynote speakers at business meetings. And Julian became a patron of The WOW! Awards.

Owing to Julian's involvement in The WOW! Awards we felt that it would not be appropriate for his people or stores to receive this award. However, in putting together this book it would be a shame to leave out Richer Sounds. Here is just one of the nominations that have been received.

Hi Derek,

Thank you for recognising my experience in the Richer Sounds Store in Brighton, now quite a few years ago.

My niece has been a resident in London now for several years. During my most recent visit I spent a day with her in London. My niece has expressed an interest in getting a CD player for the past few years and I have told her about Richer Sounds.

Since there are so many makes and models of equipment available I think she was rather reserved about shopping for something herself. I met her in London last July and we went to the Richer Sounds Swiss Cottage store as it was closest to where I was staying, although my niece lives in Walthamstow.

At the Swiss Cottage store, the manager named Lol introduced herself to us and I explained what we were looking for. My niece thought we were just looking but I knew we were there to BUY! Once again I was overcome by the same Richer Sounds 'Atmosphere' that I had experienced in Brighton a few years ago.

I bought my niece a Sherwood amp, a Kenwood 5 disc CD Deck and a pair of Eltax Speakers. We chatted with Lol for a while and even though we had just met it felt like she was an old friend we had known for years. Lol gave us 10 meters of cable and it was good quality wire too, not junk!

Now, as my niece and I discussed taking all of this stuff back to Walthamstow on the Underground (Subway to me) Lol chimed right in and happily exclaimed 'I'll take care of that for you!' She immediately called a taxi which took us from Swiss Cottage back to my niece's flat in Walthamstow. My niece was flabbergasted (gob smacked to you) and for that matter so was I.

That free taxi ride across the city of London is something we will be talking about for years!

What makes me especially happy about our day at Richer Sounds Swiss Cottage is that now my niece knows a place where she can go and feel perfectly comfortable about future purchases. (Lol the manager is a woman.)

As I put one of those Richer Sounds Virgin stickers on my niece (a little to her embarrassment) we were each presented with a free Richer Sounds Coffee Mug which believe it or not is now a cherished souvenir at my home in New York.

There is something about a Richer Sounds Shop that just makes my day! It would be a great place for depressed people to go to make them feel better. It's like going into a party everyday.

I have written about this experience to Julian Richer and he replied.

I will be in the UK again soon and can't wait to go to Richer Sounds again and I seriously mean that. I was told by my friends in the UK not to expect American Style service at many UK shops, Richer Sounds proved my friends wrong, I only wish there were a Richer Sounds here.

With thanks.

Bob Schappert
New York

What a great testimonial from Robert!

And I'm so pleased that he enjoys the service from some of the businesses in the UK.

But just when I thought that this chapter of the book was closed, I get another message from Robert.

Hi Derek,

It has been a while since I have written although I still read your WoW Award newsletters regularly. In the WoW Awards website I was reading in the Case Studies section the item titled "Guarantees & a Challenge ". This item illustrates a contributors surprise at the Richer Sounds 3 year cover plan. I learned about this quite some time ago as I always visit a Richer Sounds Shop while visiting in the UK.

My niece, who lives in the UK, is into stereo equipment and enjoying it as much as I do. When I visit she knows where her Uncle wants to go. Obviously it is not practical for me to bring all of those great deals from Richer Sounds back to the USA with me, although some of them I do. I have 'outfitted' my niece's house with many of the terrific items on sale from Richer Sounds. The first year I learned of the Richer Sounds 3 year cover plan with the money back if not used policy I bought it on some of the gifts for my niece.

After three years had come and gone on some of those 3 year cover plans, my niece followed the instructions of the cover plans and claimed the money back. I was as pleased as she was when she told me about that.

It seems nearly every electronics retailer on this side of the pond is selling 'Extended Warranties' on everything from electric can openers to computers and beyond. I seldom buy them myself as there is no deal like Richer Sounds' that is available in the UK. Whenever a retail sales person begins to give me the sales pitch about purchasing 'an Extended Warranty' on something, I always give them a reverse sales pitch and describe to them the money back if not used plan offered by Richer Sounds in the UK. I even offer them the Richer Sounds website address so they can verify I am telling them the truth and that I also have near first hand experience in claiming the money back! Yes, it really is true. After telling them this, I close with saying, 'You know the Brits really have a better idea when it comes to Extended Warranties.'

I hope to once again visit the UK later this year.

Regards,

Bob Schappert
New York, USA

What I really love about this story is not just the fabulous service that the people at Richer Sounds are giving.

And it's not just that they are helping to improve our reputation around the world.

What I really love is Bob's enthusiasm for great service. Just think about how much time he spends sharing his experiences with me, his friends and even other suppliers.

Customers really can be our greatest asset. And The WOW! Awards gives them an opportunity to say when we are doing things right. But if we don't give customers that opportunity then all we will ever get will be complaints.

A Holiday Saved –
Brown & Gammons, Baldock

Here's what Chris Lever, told us about Brown & Gammons:

"I own a 1969 MGB Roadster which we decided to use for our holiday. The plan being to drive from Aberdeen to Dover, cross over into France, drive down the west side to Biarritz, cross the Pyrenees, down to Barcelona and across to Minorca, stay a week and return, stopping in the Pyrenees again. Then make our way back to Aberdeen. 23 days in total and 3,920 miles.

We left Aberdeen on the 1st of July stopping en route at Ely for Friday and Saturday nights. Sunday morning we took off for Dover in our 1969 MGB, crossed over into France and made our first stopping point just South of Dreux, a nice chambre d'hote in the middle of nowhere but very charmingly hosted by a lady called Daggi. Next morning we moved on for our next rendezvous, a beautiful old chateau some 45 km south of Cognac.

We were about 10 km from our destination, Linda my partner was driving when I looked down at the temperature/oil pressure gauge. To my horror, the temperature gauge had gone off the scale! On looking behind we were depositing vast quantities of steam and smoke onto the road, much to the consternation of the local French drivers!! Well I thought

66

that was it, all that planning and hard work wasted, the poor old MGB was about to go back on a trailer.

Not to be beaten by these challenges and knowing that I was quite capable of completing any repair required, if at all possible. I called my MG parts supplier Brown and Gammons and was put through to Malcolm. This was now 17.40 local time - it being an hour earlier in the UK.

I explained my predicament to Malcolm and that I had blown the head gasket big time and that if I didn't get it sorted soon my other half Linda was going to be less than amused and blow hers!

No problem, he said. The gasket set was in stock and if we really all hurried this through and personally ran the package to UPS we might just get a next day delivery to the middle of France. Amazing, I thought and prayed to someone up there that it would all work out.

Malcolm called me back a little later to say that he had in fact managed to pack and despatch the parts to UPS in time to make a Next Day Delivery. I then called him back several times to talk me through some mechanical concerns.

We limped the car on 2 cylinders to the Chateau where I explained the problem to Madame and was kindly lent a barn to strip the engine down in. Next morning the engine was stripped and prepared for re-assembly. At lunch time, starting to get a bit nervous I called Malcolm, he had been tracking the package's every movement and confirmed that it was out for delivery that afternoon.

Sure enough at 16.00 hrs white van lady appeared with my valuable cargo. I rebuilt the car and we moved on at 19.30.

Much to my amazement we arrived in Biarritz at 23.00 a little late for dinner, but only 4 hrs behind schedule!! The car never missed another beat after that.

I would like to nominate Malcolm and the Brown and Gammons team for a WOW award for their help and Malcolm's going beyond the call of duty. Without their help the holiday would have been ruined."

I often talk about how suppliers and customers can work in partnership. And this is a great example.

Brown & Gammons are in business to sell parts for cars. And often that must involve shipping the parts via a courier – the cost of which is probably passed onto the customer.

So you might think that Brown & Gammons were simply doing their job.

But if they simply did their job then the parts wouldn't have made that UPS deadline.

If they simply did their job, Chris would not have been able to get the technical advice that he needed.

If they simply did their job they might not have bothered tracking the delivery.

If they simply did their job, then Chris and his partner may never have made it to Biarritz.

And you can tell from Chris's letter how important this trip was to him.

A Clean Shave – shavers.co.uk

This incredible nomination came courtesy of Jonathon Stoll:

> "I looked at shavers.co.uk's excellent website. E-mailed them for advice on whether a particular model was quieter than another.
>
> In less than an hour they e-mailed me back with a sound clip comparing the noise from three different shavers!
>
> See their website for testimonials from other satisfied customers.
>
> Does any member of staff deserve a special mention? Andrew Edwards."

WOW!

That really is something exceptional. Whilst it is easy to understand how this is possible using the latest technology, I still think that whoever came up with the idea is an absolute genius!

In Tune with the Customer – Richard Reason Pianos, Hitchin

Richard Reason Pianos of Hitchin certainly overwhelmed Belinda Gee.

Here's Belinda's story:

"When we moved last Christmas to a house that needed a lot of refurbishment we reluctantly parted company with our piano as we would be short of space for a while. The idea was that we would treat ourselves to a baby grand as soon as the room was refurbished and the builders were no longer in residence.

Nine months later we still had builders and no piano. The children's piano teacher quietly suggested that we either replace our piano or give up on lessons because lack of practice meant that they were not progressing.

We decided to go to the Richard Reason Pianos in Hitchin to see if we could negotiate buying an upright, which we could sell back when we had space for the baby grand. Obviously we were hopeful that they would agree to buy the upright back for something close to our purchase price.

Rupert Frost (owner of the business) had a better idea. He suggested we bought the baby grand we wanted, he would then keep it in his warehouse until we needed it and in the meantime he would lend us an upright - all this for no extra cost than the initial piano purchase. Fantastic offer but it gets better yet.....

The loan piano was delivered exactly on time just a few days later. It turned out to be a beautiful 25 year old Yamaha which had been on sale in the shop for more than we paid for our piano. We had been expecting Rupert to deliver an inexpensive piano that nobody wanted to buy (we would still have been more than delighted) but to have such a high quality instrument on indefinite loan is fantastic. We are overwhelmed!

Lest any sceptics think that this is a clever bit of 'puppy dog' selling, Rupert is well aware that we love the baby grand and can't wait to put it into its new home!

Anybody interested in pianos should take the opportunity to drop into this shop - it is fascinating. It is very old, has beautiful beams, double doors open out of the first floor where there is a Victorian lift used for hoisting the pianos up. The ground floor is used as shop and workshop and there is always somebody there in the middle of stripping down a piano for refurbishment.

Almost forgot, Rupert made me a coffee whilst the paperwork was sorted out - seems so insignificant against the overall picture but how many other shops would have done that?"

This story about the piano certainly makes for a fantastic nomination. But isn't it interesting how the cup of coffee also made such a great impression on Belinda. In this era of busy lives and supermarkets it's easy to forget how something as simple as a cup of coffee can make such a big difference.

Honest Customers – Ken's Fine Art Galleries

"Nick Tye at Keen's Fine Art Galleries didn't know me but he chose to trust me."

Angie Court is Director of Customer Service at Avis Europe Plc. Angie certainly knows what makes good service and how important it is. So getting a nomination from Angie is praise indeed. Here's what Angie told me about Nick Tye at Keen's Fine Art Galleries:

"I went into this shop with 2 minutes to closing time to get a birthday present for that evening. I knew what I wanted as I had bought one of the limited prints by this artist from them 3 years earlier, and they had a full selection at that time.

Nick greeted me warmly and I spluttered out what I wanted but I couldn't remember the artist's name but I assured him I would know as soon as I saw it.

Unbeknown to me - the gallery had changed hands during the last 3 years. So it was different stock. Also they had only just reopened the previous week following a terrible car accident which smashed into their gallery ruining huge amounts of stock.

It was touch and go whether they would even be stocking the same artist and, if they did stock him, they might not have any available for me to take for the birthday present.

Nick spent over three quarters of an hour looking with me. We found one. Well we think we did but I wasn't sure. This is then the real wow factor: he let me take it without paying and without leaving my name or address! Nick didn't know me but he chose to trust me. This is not a backwater in the country where people leave their back doors open - this is nearly London!

The picture was fine - phew. I phoned Nick the following day and said I could pay over the phone and thank you etc. I said I would be in on Saturday to arrange framing. He still didn't want any money and said Saturday would be fine.

I have now been in to arrange framing and guess what - he still doesn't want any money till I go to collect it!!

Well you know where I will buy all my pictures from and also where I will be recommending people to go.

He is also a really nice bloke who loves what he does. I truly hope no one spoils that for him, and he will always meet honest customers."

Nick was delighted to be invited to The WOW! Awards very first conference where Angie presented him with his certificate.

Trusting the Customer – Robert Ritchie of Montrose, Scotland.

Here's what one of their customers had to say.

"I went to Robert Ritchie in December looking for some replacement hi-fi speakers, and hoping to arrange a home demonstration in the next week or two. Not only were they extremely helpful on Saturday (lots of time taken, coffee provided, etc) but I was sent home with two pairs of brand new speakers, value over £1000, to try out, and with no pressure to return them quickly. They did not know me, and refused the deposit I offered.

This was followed by a visit from Mr Ritchie Senior, early on Sunday evening. This was extremely helpful in enabling me to decide which speaker was best for my room. I still needed time to decide, however, and was allowed to keep them longer with no firm date for their return. I eventually contacted them on Tuesday, when they were happy to let me retain the unwanted speakers until they were next in the area. However, I took them back to Montrose on Wednesday, to square up. Not only was I presented with another coffee, but also had a further hour's relaxed chat with Mr Ritchie, and a demonstration of some equipment that was way out of my league but fun to listen to. I left feeling that I wasn't a customer, but a friend.

After Mr Ritchie left on Sunday evening, my wife (not a hi-fi enthusiast) said, "Now I see why people keep going back to that chap. You'll never get service like that anywhere else." I related my experience on the e-mail forum of a well-known hi-fi manufacturer, and within the hour four or five other posts came in describing similar experiences, over many years, which others had had while dealing with Mr Ritchie. The general consensus was that he is the best hi-fi dealer in Scotland."

WOW! What a great story.

We at The WOW! Awards were seriously impressed. The award is thoroughly deserved.

I wrote to Robert Ritchie to tell him about the nomination. First thing next morning he was on the phone to say 'thank you'. Robert's passion and enthusiasm is addictive. So if you're ever in Montrose and want hi-fi, Robert Ritchie is your man.

Presenting Robert with his certificate was going to be a big problem for me. Robert Ritchie is in Montrose, Scotland. And I'm based just a few miles north of London. So how could I deliver Robert's WOW! Award certificate to him?

Then I hit on the idea of asking David Robb to help me. David kindly agreed to do the honours for me and to take some pictures that we could incorporate into a press release.

But David was in for a further surprise. When he went along to make the presentation Robert took David out to lunch to celebrate the award! WOW!

WOW! Beyond the Customer –
Harris Lipman, North London

Here's what Harris Lipman incorporate into their way of doing business:-

1. Annual prize for the team member giving best service of £1000 to their favourite charity.

2. Constant personal development for all team members.

3. Cleaning client cars.

4. Getting team members involved in the recruitment process.

5. Comments from customers about "helpful and energetic in responding to any question"

6. Ingrained philosophy of service as reported by team members.

7. Birthday cakes for clients that came into the office.

8. "Whatever it takes" attitude

9. Vision summed up in acronym of RESPECT.

The decision to give The WOW! Award to Harris Lipman was really a no-brainer. I had already heard a year or so ago about this firm's policy of washing client's cars. My bank manager, Nicky Kleanthous, had been to visit Harris Lipman and had her car cleaned. Nicky phoned me up especially to tell me about it but never officially nominated Harris Lipman for an award.

Well done Howard Jackson and all the Team at Harris Lipman. You got your award in the end.

Follow up:

After presenting The WOW! Awards I always hope that the service standards will be maintained. I want other people to experience exactly the same great service that I've seen.

Some months after Harris Lipman received their award, I had the privilege to visit their offices in Whetstone, North London.

Having phoned to make the appointment, I got this letter.

Dear Mr Williams,

I have been advised by Howard that you are visiting our offices on Friday 19 October at 2.00 p.m. and I am writing to you to see whether you would like to accept our offer of having your car valeted whilst you are attending our offices, at our expense.

Whilst we make every effort to visit our clients wherever possible, I am sure you can appreciate that it is a significant time saving to us when clients such as yourself do take the time and effort to visit us, and we felt that we would like to offer this service as a token of our appreciation.

I shall call you within the next two to three days to see whether you would like to accept our offer.

I trust that you will appreciate that this offer is conditional upon prevailing weather conditions.

Yours sincerely

Sarah O'Brien
Client Welfare Officer

I spoke to Sarah a few days later and explained that I was not a proper client and so I'd not be taking up her kind offer. 'I don't see as that matters,' said Sarah. 'I think that you should have it done anyway.'

But that was just part of the story.

I was also dazzled by a wonderful reception area with music playing softly in the background. Sarah was absolutely wonderful. There were lovely displays of flowers and a Team Commitment on the wall left me in no doubt that this was an extraordinary business.

When asked if I'd like a drink I requested some water. Two beautiful blue glass, chilled bottles of water appeared. One still and one sparkling. A stunning cut glass tumbler was placed on a drinks coaster ready for me to use.

And when I came out of the building, there was my car – sparkling clean and positioned ready for me to drive away.

WOW!

And what is Harris Lipman's business? They're a firm of accountants! Not normally a business that you'd associate with customer service but they're setting a standard that is way beyond the norm for any business.

So what can you learn from this?

Harris Lipman stunned me with first impressions – the letter and the reception. And what a fantastic letter it is. Just take a moment to read it again the way a customer would.

They dazzled me with second impressions – the reception area, the Team Commitment, the water bottles, the music and the flowers.

They blew my mind with the last impressions. Not only was my car clean but it was lined up ready to drive away!

What first, second and last impressions are you creating?

Just be Patient! The Stroke Unit, Lister Hospital, Stevenage

Colin Marvell was only 40 but was unfortunate to suffer a stroke and was admitted to The Stroke Unit at Lister Hospital.

Colin's work experience has given him the ability to recognise outstanding service. He has worked in customer service for many years in the banking sector. Colin is also a member of The Institute of Customer Service.

This is what Colin had to tell us:

"The Stroke Unit is a wonderful place. The treatment is fantastic – every patient is treated as an individual by the team and made to feel that they are the centre of their universe.

Everyone involved in the care of the stroke patient, from consultants, nurses, physiotherapists and occupational therapists, meets together with the patient regularly to discuss their treatment and progress.

This includes the patient setting goals with a timetable in mind and then working with the team on how to achieve the goals. For example, I wanted to be able to climb stairs by a certain date and we all worked together on an action plan so that I could do this.

Families are encouraged to visit for 'Family Question Time' so that treatment and tests and the reasons for them can be discussed and explained clearly and fully.

A special mention for Sarah Brogden the Unit Coordinator. Sarah knew that I had a customer service background, and asked me to design a customer service questionnaire for patients to complete when they are discharged.

Even the food was good!"

The things that Colin described as being great service in a hospital ward are <u>every bit as relevant to any business.</u> Read the points again and see how you could apply these to what you do for your customers.

I was especially thrilled to present this award for a number of reasons:-

Stevenage is my home town. So it was really nice to be able to do something positive for my town.

Colin Marvell is such a great character – his energy and enthusiasm are fantastic. I wish him a full and speedy recovery.

The Lister Hospital had come in for a lot of criticism at that time. The hospital did not do well in a government report and there was even more bad news in the local papers.

When an organisation comes in for criticism, we sometimes lose sight of the fact that an organisation consists of people. These people are totally committed to their work and they have feelings.

In the UK the National Health Service has suffered from a lack of investment in people, training and equipment. We need to remember that most people are doing the best that they can with the resources that they have available to them.

The reaction that we got from the Team at The Stroke Unit when Colin and I went along to present this award was unbelievable. The atmosphere was absolutely electric. You could feel the enthusiasm of these people. They were so thrilled to have been nominated. Everyone was there – the doctors, nurses, therapists and even the Chief Executive.

I was greeted with a choice of drinks and a range of lovely cakes – all laid on by the Team.

The local papers were there as well as the press officer from the Institute of Customer Service.

I was able to spend some quality time with this Team hearing about the help that they gave Colin and to all the patients in their care. I felt almost embarrassed. Such a simple certificate seemed such small reward for what these people do.

Sarah Brogden told me: "We are absolutely thrilled to receive this award. It means even more to us because a patient nominated us for the award because they felt that we provided a good service. The staff at the stroke unit work extremely hard for the patients that we care for and by setting them goals for their recovery not only does the patient feel a sense of achievement but so do we."

Afterwards I reflected some more on what had happened. And I wondered about the power of The WOW! Awards. It might not be nearly as significant as a "government report" but which one will do the most good?

Which one will inspire the people that work there to give great service?

Service You Can See! – Guellers Restaurant, Leeds

How often have you gone out to a restaurant, the cinema or even just shopping and realise that you've forgotten your glasses?

Phil Turner wrote to tell me how he discovered a very special detail of the customer service at Guellers Restaurant in Leeds.

> "I visited this week to speak to Rena Gueller - she had just been speaking to a sales rep and had lent him some glasses as he had forgotten his own.
>
> It turns out that Rena always keeps a few pairs of standard prescription glasses in her office just in case any customers who are reading their menu have forgotten their glasses - a little touch of customer service but an excellent one as well."

It's exactly this sort of attention to detail that I love.

Someone has come up with this as an idea and implemented it. So often, people spot a problem or have an idea but never do anything about implementing it. Full marks to Guellers.

And what does it tell you about the quality of the soup at Guellers Restaurant? Having taken so much care to help their customers read the menu, don't you think that they are likely to take a lot of care over the soup?

French Maid – Scholes of Battersea

Mike Ogilvie is a Profit Coach and sent me this WOW! story.

In my coaching these days I try to persuade teams to think of themselves as "WOW extraction machines" in order to get them to assume the mindset I am after from them.

I recently visited one of my London clients, an Interior Designer called Jill Damaris Scholes from Battersea. While discussing their affairs, her assistant Sally explained a recent "WOW" moment they had created following my last meeting with them.

They had been commissioned to redesign a client's kitchen.

At the end of the job, when the client moved back in, he found the fridge fully stocked and a note from Sally in the fridge saying, "Sorry we could not provide the French Maid, but you should find everything else in the fridge (including Bottle of Champagne and orange juice for Bucks Fizz) to enjoy your first breakfast in your new kitchen".

Needless to say, their client was 'wowed', and Jill and Sally were delighted with the extra impact created by this little extra thought. And hopefully, extracting that WOW! may lead to many referrals from that customer.

It's a great story Mike. I really like the idea of WOW! Extraction Machines. This is a simple idea that every business could pick up on.

Extra Care – Waitrose, Welwyn Garden City.

Roger Stephens sent me this fabulous nomination for The WOW! Award.

Waitrose is part of the John Lewis Group and, as we know from previous experience, they are reluctant to accept our awards. But the story is another fantastic example from one of the UK's best loved retailers.

"My wife Edna has a favourite Aunt who is 84, and who is beginning to cause us concern because her memory lets her down more and more.

The other day, Aunt Lil wanted to get her shoes mended and Edna had other things she just had to do that morning. So she dropped Lil at the Howard Centre and arranged to meet her at such-and-such time by the escalator on the ground floor.

Come the appointed hour and no sign of Lil.

A worried Edna thinks – "ah, she's probably in Marks & Spencer." And starts a patrol up and down the mall: no sign of Lil. She alerts the security people to the problem so that she can feel comfortable going across and looking for Lil in John Lewis - another favourite hunting ground for Lil when she comes down from the Midlands to visit us.

Still no sign. By now more than an hour has gone by and Edna's beginning to get very worried indeed. Police are alerted.

After two hours, with no reports of any old ladies lost & wandering, Edna decides to go back to our house in Lemsford, just in case Lil has somehow gone there under her own steam.

There, sitting out at the back is Lil and her new toy-boy, the Manager of Waitrose. Apparently, she had realised she'd forgotten where the rendezvous was supposed to be, and had taken herself over to Waitrose because she knew Edna did most of her food shopping here. She'd sat in one of those seats by the checkouts, asking anyone she could whether they knew where her niece (who shopped there a lot) lived. She'd forgotten the address.

Eventually, the staff got worried enough to call in the boss, and Lil managed to remember that Edna (who's 60 herself) lived somewhere near the bottom of Valley Road where "you go under that railway bridge."

So what does this lovely man do? He puts her in his car and goes down to the end of Valley Road. There isn't a railway bridge, but there is a motorway bridge, and as soon as he drives through, Lil says "THAT's Edna's house over there." Then it becomes clear that she hasn't got a key, so he stays with her. She walks him round the garden. And he stays with her till her niece arrives.

Then when he's thanked he has the grace to say he hasn't enjoyed a lunch hour so much for years and years...

WOW! Fabulous story and well worth reporting to every potential Waitrose customer!

The Show after the Show! – Sarastro Restaurant, Drury Lane, London

It was June, 2003 when we received this nomination from Rosie Piper.

"I booked a table for five persons for lunch at Sarastro on Sunday 4th May, as we had tickets for the matinee performance of 'Night of 1000 Voices' at the Royal Albert Hall.

As some of us in the party were working to limited budgets I had chosen the 'tenor' (£10) menu to include starter or dessert and main course only. £10 for a meal in the heart of 'theatre land' is very reasonable.

I had never eaten at Sarastro before, but I had seen their advertisements in theatre programmes. When seated at our table the waiter approached us and offered to 'upgrade' our meal to the Roast Lamb (normally £17.50) at no extra cost. The meal was delicious, perfectly cooked and the free entertainment (opera singers) made the event really special.

On the following day (Bank Holiday Monday), three of us decided that we had enjoyed our lunch so much that we would return to Sarastro for lunch again that day, so my friend telephoned and booked a table IN A DIFFERENT NAME.

On arrival, the headwaiter not only remembered us, but also offered to seat us at the same table we had occupied previously. We again enjoyed a delicious meal from the 'tenor' menu, one person opting for a starter and main course, and two for main course and dessert.

When the dessert menu arrived, the lady who had chosen a starter decided that she REALLY must have the Crème Brûlée, and asked for one to be added as an 'extra' to our bill. After the meal we ordered coffee, and the headwaiter asked us to accept a complimentary liqueur 'on the house' to go with our coffee.

The final icing on the cake was that when the bill arrived, the charge for the 'extra' dessert was for the cheapest of the three - not the Crème Brûlée, which was the dearest.

Needless to say, I am recommending Sarastro to EVERYONE I meet!"

Whilst this nomination was excellent we could never have foreseen how the story would unfold.

Rosie's description sounded like a great story to us. Colin Marvell, who was helping me with processing WOW! Award entries, called Sarastro to tell them the news.

Sometimes we have some difficulty convincing nominated businesses that we are genuine. They seem to suspect that this is some sort of con or that they've got to pay for the award. But not in this case!

I was sat in the office next to Colin as he made the call. I could immediately tell that Colin was having loads of fun speaking to the owner of Sarastro. And then it got to the bit where Colin said that we would write and confirm the award, who should we write to? 'King Richard' was the reply!

'But I can't write to King Richard,' says Colin. 'Don't you have a surname?'

'No,' came the reply. 'Just write to King Richard and it will find me.'

Colin and I laughed our socks off. What sort of crazy people were we dealing with here?

Colin had arranged to present the certificate on Friday morning at Sarastro which is on the corner of London's Drury Lane - right in the heart of 'theatre land'. But I couldn't make it myself. I had another appointment in London that day and so I left it in Colin's capable hands.

Come the day of the presentation and my meeting finished a little earlier than I'd expected. I switched on my mobile phone to pick up my messages and the very first message was from an extremely excited Colin. 'I'm at Sarastro! I've had a banquet and I'm on Turkish TV! Get over here if you can!'

I jumped in the first taxi I could and asked him to get to Drury Lane as quick as possible. And was I glad that I did.

King Richard came out to meet me on the pavement as the taxi pulled up.

I was immediately struck by the exterior. I saw a fabulous display of colour, lush green plants and fabulous hanging baskets of flowers. Beautiful crimson and gold sofas. An entrance doorway that was open and inviting. There was the sound of opera music and the aroma of fabulous food. The waiters were perfectly dressed - crisp white shirts and aprons, beautiful black waistcoats and bow ties, immaculately groomed and with perfect welcoming smiles.

I was being seriously WOWed! and I hadn't even got inside yet. Every one of my senses was aware that this was going to be a very special experience.

A film crew appeared and started work. There was so much going on all at once, total chaos!

I was ushered into the restaurant. I was hit by the colour, the music, the detail the vibrancy. This was just fabulously overwhelming.

Whilst being interviewed for Turkish TV, a menu appeared along with huge bowls of fresh breads, tropical fruit, delicious dips, pineapples, strawberries, cheeses. WOW! WOW! WOW!

I sat back and tried to soak up the experience.

Balconies decorated to resemble theatre boxes added another tier of seats - cosy areas that were clearly fun (and accommodated more customers).

Michaelangelo must have spent some time here. The ceiling was an artistic masterpiece.

Fabulous Turkish rugs, vases, lamps, embroidery and art decorated every inch of this fabulous, fabulous place. Sights, sounds and smells in a fabulous swirl.

Turkish TV presenter, Aynur Sezer, joined us at our table. Her beauty and lovely Turkish accent brought perfection.

As I sat there trying to take it all in, Colin lent across the table. 'How would you describe how you feel about Sarastro?' he asked me.

I thought for a moment. I remembered reading a piece by Tom Peters about how every town seems to have a profusion of shops and restaurants. "How people work so hard to launch something new, only to create a business that is so ordinary. The passion is missing. So is the soul. There's nothing to make you say 'WOW' or 'Great' or make you want to change your life. You don't fall in love."

My senses sucked in another cocktail of the Sarastro atmosphere. I lent forward and said, 'Colin, I'm in love!'

But it didn't end there!

I reported the story in The WOW! Awards newsletter and stared getting even more stories about Sarastro.

It soon became clear that some of our readers had known about Sarastro for a while and had been keeping it a secret! But that doesn't surprise me - when a place is this good you almost want to keep it especially for yourself.

Here's what Andy Esson (now living in New York) told me:

> "I was fascinated to read your piece about Sarastro, as I have been taking friends and clients there for many years, so I guess its just one of those places that you assume everyone has been to....! Great place...!"

But then I got this absolutely amazing message from Sharon Keefe:

> "I too have been to Sarastro Restaurant and whole heartedly applaud the fact that they have received the WOW award.
>
> My experience was equally uplifting in terms of excellent customer service.
>
> On the evening that I visited Sarastro I was expecting an important business call on my mobile. Sarastro is great in terms of food and ambience and there is a real buzz of excitement but it is not the place to take a call on a mobile...............you just cannot hear the caller.
>
> So when the call came I walked outside the restaurant and took the call in the street.
>
> As I was talking, the manager of the restaurant approached me and pointed to a Rolls Royce that was parked outside of the restaurant. He then opened the door of the Rolls Royce and waved me into it. Once I was sitting inside the Rolls, the manager very kindly set out a desk for me including pen and paper and also offered me champagne whilst I was on the call.

I can tell you this is the way to do business!

Now when I think of Sarastro, my mind goes back to not only the food and the atmosphere but the fact that they went that the extra mile to make me comfortable.

Now that is what I call great customer service!"

Isn't that just the most incredible story you've ever heard?

I gave my readers this latest update. And started thinking about all the special people in my life and how I'd just love them to try Sarastro too. And in the years since that first nomination I have visited Sarastro many, many times with friends, family and business colleagues.

My favourite place to sit within the restaurant is in a seat facing the doorway. That way, I can watch people entering the restaurant.

There are two types of people.

Those who have been before are warmly welcomed back.

And then there are those who have not been before.

These people usually stand in the doorway and gaze open mouthed at this incredible place. And then there mouths move in such a way that I can see they are saying just one word. 'WOW!'

But it didn't end there.

In 2005 I had a call from Brian Milligan, TV presenter wit the BBC. Brian wanted to know if there was somewhere that I could recommend in London. Somewhere where the service was outstanding and would make a good feature for an upcoming news item.

Of course, I recommended Sarastro. And Sarastro was featured on BBC Breakfast News. This is exactly what I had always hoped for with The WOW! Awards; that people would look to the very best and aspire to be like them.

But it didn't end there.

Over the years, I've told the Sarastro story to literally thousands of people through my newsletters and in my businesses presentations.

On one occasion, I was making a presentation to a group of business people. And I told the story of Sarastro but without actually saying whereabouts the restaurant was.

At the end of my presentation, I was approached by Gavin Brooking. He and his colleague were going to be staying London that evening and asked if I could recommend this restaurant for them to have a meal.

I emphasised that I had no relationship with the restaurant other than that they were a past winner of The WOW! Awards. However, I suggested that, when they arrived at the restaurant, they let them know that they had been recommended by me. And just see what happens.

The next day, I received an email from Gavin. And this is what he had to say:

"Hi Derek

It was good to meet you again on the 25th of April, Mark and I thoroughly enjoyed the day.

You may remember me saying we were staying in London that night and a group of us ate at Sarastro which we all thought was extremely good.

I mentioned that you had recommended us to go there and they brought us 2 bottles of wine with their compliments saying one was from you and one from them.

I wasn't quite sure how that transpired but thought you might shine some light on the matter. Anyway it was very impressive so thank you!"

Kind Regards

Gavin Brooking
Forest Products

WOW!

Sarastro blows my mind again!

So, two days later, I drop by Sarastro and offer to pay for the bottle of wine. I'm not going to tell you what they said. I'll leave you to guess.

I have a feeling that it doesn't end here.

Footnote: Sarastro and Papageno (King Richard's other restaurant just two blocks away) are named after characters in Mozart's opera The Magic Flute.

Sarastro symbolises the reasonable sovereign who rules with paternalistic wisdom and enlightened insight. A perfect description for King Richard.

'So long, and thanks for all the goldfish' – Kings Estate Agents, Hatfield

Lorraine and David Hughes let their estate agent take care of tricky fish-for-fittings negotiations while they were on holiday and were delighted with the service they got. Here's what they had to say about Kings Estate Agents at Hatfield.

> "Can we really bring ourselves to nominate an estate agent for a WOW award? Normally, no! But Kings (partners Tyron King and Ann O'Connor) are really different.
>
> Apart from doing what all estates agents do, only better, they have introduced a number of innovations to the business such as honesty, humour and good client communications. However, these alone would not really justify a WOW. It is the optional extras that distinguish Kings.
>
> During our recent property sale, not only did they successfully negotiate a good price (their job, of course), they also negotiated on our behalf the sale of kitchen appliances and we must not forget the fish!
>
> Whilst we were on vacation and at a critical stage (nothing like getting your priorities right) they organised and confirmed for us the removals and storage contractors.
>
> These guys really do deserve a WOW!"

It's a great story from Lorraine and David. But everyone who I have told this story to has asked about the fish. And so, when I went along to the presentation of their certificate, I had to check with Ann O'Connor. 'What was the full story on the fish?'

It turns out that Lorraine and David had to leave Ann to conclude the negotiations over fixtures and fittings. And Ann successfully managed to negotiate a trade of window blinds for goldfish. It might seem like a trivial detail but it's this sort of attention to detail that customers really love.

A Moving Experience – Gray's Removals, Muswell Hill

You might be in tears if you find the removal men pulling apart your cupboard, but when confronted with this sight, one customer was delighted with the team's dedication to moving the unit around a snug corner.

Here's what we heard from customer Andrea Tynan. She said:

> "Not only were Grays Removals competitively priced, but also they were helpful, polite and really wanted to help me when I called them.
>
> I was armed with limited information about some rubbish that needed removing from two locations and disposing of at the rubbish tip. I also needed them to collect some exhibition equipment from a locked storage facility and bring it back to our office (I had not seen this exhibition equipment and had no idea how much there was or what it was. All I was able to tell them was that our storage area was 40 feet square.)
>
> On the day, they showed up on time and smiling. They removed all of our rubbish and disposed of it for us.
>
> Then they collected our exhibition equipment, which turned out to be timber wall panels of over six feet in height, an

enormous, sturdily constructed cupboard and a very large transportation box which contained posters and promotional material and numerous other boxes.

They worked hard all afternoon, getting these items up five, very narrow flights of stairs; our offices are in a very old building above shops on a busy High Street.

When they finally got to the last item, the sturdy cupboard, they tried every which way to get up the first flight of stairs and around the corner, but to no avail. At 7.00 p.m., which was later than we were all anticipating working, we stood back and looked at the problem.

Well, I say we looked at the problem. The outstanding thing was that THEY looked at their problem! It was never, for one moment my problem. I needed to get this cupboard upstairs and it simply would not fit. Rather than say to me, 'We're very sorry it's not possible to do', they considered the possibilities, it had become their problem and they were determined to find a solution.

The cupboard was too heavy to lift over the banisters, but could not be dismantled because I no longer had the key to the doors; they spent some time trying to manually unlock the doors to no avail.

They suggested I contact the cabinet maker the following day to obtain a spare key and they would come back a day later, dismantle the cupboard, take it upstairs and then reassemble it at no extra charge, because that was my need – to get it upstairs.

How outstanding, I found it hard to believe that these guys, that had worked so hard all day, were willing to come back and spend another few hours working to 'solve my problem'!

The cabinet maker managed to get two of the three doors open. And, as promised, the guys from Grays turned up the following day, removed the two doors and top of the cupboard in the confines of our narrow entrance hall. Making it lighter, they then struggled for another couple of hours to get the still very heavy body of the cupboard up to the top floor and finally reassembled it for us.

We really can't thank them enough for putting in so much effort, we would have had such a problem with the large cupboard and it would have had to go back into storage, but for their determination.

And did I mention they even re-hung one of our pictures for us on their way out? The hook had come loose and needed hammering back in to the wall. What stars!"

That's what we're looking for! Dedication beyond the call of duty and a desire to delight the customer has earned Gray's Removals of London a WOW! Award and our admiration.

Getting the Star Treatment – Hollywood Hair

Hollywood Hair made Jennifer Reefe feel like a film star.

Jennifer Reefe looked a million dollars after her visit to Hollywood Hair. Here's what Jennifer told me:

"I was encouraged by my dear friend to change my hairdresser and book an appointment with hers, who she thought was great. As I value her opinion, and after she took me in, I made an appointment for the next day.

I was a little apprehensive. However, from the moment I walked in I was welcomed by friendly faces, offered refreshment, and my coat was taken. The place itself has a wonderful feeling, very relaxing. All the members of staff were smiling and friendly.

I was then taken to my stylist Janine who sat with me and discussed what I would like to change and how to take care of my hair after the cut. She took lots of time making me feel comfortable. After we talked and had decided on my new style I was taken to have my hair washed.

Every client gets a new towel, opened from the packet. Whilst you have your hair washed you are offered the footrest which massages your feet. By this time I was in heaven! They were making me feel wonderful.

I was talked through my haircut every step of the way so I felt reassured (I get nervous with haircuts). The result was very special. I looked years younger. I was given what I had asked for - to look completely different. I was amazed, I felt great and now I get compliments every day.

Janine asked if I might like to come back for a colour, which I booked then and there and was told it would be half price. WOW!

When I left they gave me a single yellow rose, and two handmade chocolates. WOW! again. I felt fantastic and still do.

I am so impressed with all the staff. They receive regular training which sounds fantastic and are all very good at their job and are very happy. I have never felt so good at any hairdressers I have ever been to.

I now look forward to my next visit and of course I have been telling everyone to go there. Maxine is delightful and made sure I was welcomed and looked after. She really takes time to care and make you feel special. I would highly recommend Hollywood and hope you feel they are special enough for one of your WOW awards."

WOW!
that's what i call service!

Exceeding Expectations – Little Things

This section is about the extraordinary attention to detail that some businesses go to. Lots of little things.

Little things that many people might not even think about.

Little things that some people might not even notice.

But when people do notice little things, those little things can often have a profound effect on the customer.

Working on the Frontline

Linda Green runs the ticket office at Redcar Railway Station for Northern Rail. She started at the station in 1983 when it was still British Rail and after six years working at Middlesbrough Station, she returned to Redcar after the birth of her first daughter in 1988 and now runs the office single handed.

With a huge personality and great love for life and her job, Linda is one of those people whose helpful, friendly manner makes them naturals for customer facing roles. Linda brings so much extra to her role that she has become well known in her small town as the friendly lady 'that sorts out the trains' and is admired and respected amongst the local railway community, including those working for other rail operating companies who seek her advice and knowledge.

Such is Linda's reputation that people prefer being served by Linda, even if they have to wait whilst she deals with others, rather than order by telephone or internet and elderly people ask when she is taking her holidays so that they can book their travel with her rather than book when she is away.

Linda is an ambassador and her story demonstrates the impact that one person can have on customers if organisations can get their recruitment, motivation and job satisfaction right.

Linda's story probably starts with her pride in her town. Redcar is a small north-eastern coastal town with a population of 40,000. Not far from the station is the town centre with its famous town centre clock tower and beyond the tower lies a wonderful beach that stretches five miles to Saltburn in one direction and five miles to Seaton Carew in the other. The area also boasts a famous racecourse that brings plenty of business to the area and Linda is particularly busy on race days.

Linda does everything at the station so that while selling tickets is her main function she also cleans the office, the floor and the toilets, offers travel advice, helps with luggage, informs passengers of delays and gives directions to arriving passengers.

Greeting everyone with a smile, Linda knows many of her customers by name; both those who use the service regularly and those who just make occasional trips to visit their relations in other parts of the country.

She has built up her relationships with her customers over many years and with other railway groups, including user groups, action groups, enthusiasts and railway professionals. 'They know me and I know them,' she says with a smile and uses that knowledge to help them whenever she can.

She might spot that a regular traveller might be better off financially with a season ticket, even if he or she does not travel every day. She knows that they might not realise this and points it out to them in conversation when they next purchase a ticket.

Elderly customers look to Linda to help them with their travel arrangements when visiting sons and daughters 'down south'. 'What are the best days and times to travel?' they ask, knowing that Linda will be aware not only of all pricing implications but of the quieter times when the journey will be easier. She will often recommend the best places to change to elderly customers, avoiding the big and potentially intimidating junctions such as Birmingham Central for smaller quieter stations such as Bristol Parkway.

Customers love that sort of attention to their needs and Linda is often confronted by 'I'm off to see our Rita again, can I buy my ticket?' Sometimes, because it may have been a year ago and Linda has lots of customers, she may not instantly recall where Rita lives but often rather than admit this straight away, a few questions about the previous journey will enable Linda to work out the destination rather than ask the question directly.

Understanding customers has enabled Linda to remove their fears of travelling. For example if she knows the connection may be tight for an elderly or disabled customer, she will look up the time of the next train and say, 'Don't worry if you miss the connection, it is only forty minutes before the one after that, time to have a nice cup of tea and find the platform.' Linda knows that for these passengers such reassurance is more important than a bit of lost time.

As well as helping elderly and disabled customers with their luggage, she will phone ahead where appropriate and arrange for a porter to be on hand to help at the destination.

At times trains can be late and passengers can get annoyed. Linda always meets this front on. Rather than relying just on public address announcements, she will walk along the platform at the earliest opportunity and explain as much as she can about the delay. Even where she does not know the final outcome as to when the train will arrive, she will still give as much information as she can as soon as she can to keep her customers informed.

She has even been known, when a severe delay is occurring, to ring some of her commuters and advise them to stay in bed for an extra half hour before departing for the station! Also when trains are late she offers to ring offices for customers to warn their colleagues. On one occasion, some years ago, when the service was going through a difficult period, she wrote a letter on a young lady's behalf to her boss who doubted her excuses for regular late arrival.

Like so many great service providers, Linda regularly goes beyond what is asked of her. Every year, assisted by her family, she installs a Christmas tree in the station office, decorated in the company colours. The tree and decorations are provided at Linda's expense and it has become a family tradition to install the tree on a Sunday before Christmas on Linda's day off.

Some years ago, she saw a 1930s poster of Redcar in a shop in another town. She bought it for herself but decided to put it up in the booking office ('I spend more time there than I do at home.') So many customers commented upon it and asked where they could buy one, that she purchased a supply of nine different prints and sold them all over an 18 month period, making a small profit for the railway company but, more importantly, providing an extra service and topic of conversation for her customers.

As well as the day job, Linda has volunteered to be involved in two special units. One is CATS – Customer Action Team – that can be parachuted in to special situations where severe delays resulting from signal failures or a derailment may mean that an outlying station or stranded train may need extra staff to help customers.

She is also a member of the Major Rail Incident Care Team that is set up to respond to real emergencies such as a major crash or terrorist incident. She is happy to attend the various training days where simulated exercises are carried out but fervently hopes that she will never be required to attend a real incident.

One of her reasons for volunteering for this role was that many years ago, she was stuck on a failed tube train in London and she had to walk along the lines under the tunnel to safety. Although there was no actual danger, it was dark, cold and eerie. The wind whistling through the tunnel made it sound like a train was coming towards them but the railwayman that led them out was calm and reassuring. Linda has never forgotten that experience and whilst hoping that she will never be needed, Linda would be the very person, apart from the emergency professionals, that customers would want on hand.

Meeting Linda and listening to her story, brings back memories of the golden age of the railways. If all customer service professionals were like Linda, there would not be a great need for training or books like this.

The Grand Hotel – Eastbourne

This nomination comes from The Profit Team. They have been great supporters of The WOW! Awards.

We run a monthly breakfast business meeting, 'The Business Builder Forum for Entrepreneurs' at the Grand Hotel.

Every month, Michael Ogilvie and his secretary Pippa turn up at about 7.20 a.m. and are always greeted in the car park by Jamieson, the duty manager, who offers to help carry in any of our equipment and papers.

Once Michael was really keen and arrived early at 7.05 am and was amazed to find Jamieson running out to help, concerned that he had nearly been caught out. It just makes you think - with all the work he has to do as duty manager, what sort of customer care system does he have to ensure that he personally meets us when we arrive?

This month we were greeted, as usual, but were told that as it was the 20th meeting we had held there, they were offering our members complimentary champagne or bucks fizz with their breakfast.

Needless to say, not only were we wowed but so were our members, who are now looking forward to Champagne on their 21st, 22nd etc.... meetings.

We would like to nominate Jamieson and The Grand Hotel for a WOW award.

Such a nice and unexpected touch. Just what The WOW! Awards are all about.

As easy as... ABC Music – Hounslow

When Helen Kalyan's 8 year old son started learning to play the cello, his teacher recommended a book for his lessons and to practise with.

"I tried several music stores and websites over a period of 6 weeks to find the book without success. One Saturday afternoon I passed ABC music and thought I would have one last-ditch attempt and called in.

From the moment I opened the door I received fantastic service, with a cheerful good morning. I asked for the book, and Tony checked his stock and when he didn't have it, he called two other shops to see if they had a copy. Still without success he took my name and number and promised to call his supplier and order it for me as soon as it was open on Monday.

Tony also promised to call me on Monday and confirm the order. I duly received a call on Monday at 10 a.m., explaining that he could not find this book at all and could it be possible that I had the wrong title? (He explained very diplomatically.) Being sure that I had the right title he then asked for the author.

Later that day he called again and said that he had finally found the book. He politely explained that I did indeed have the wrong title. He then asked if I wanted the book posted to me, postage complimentary or if I wanted to collect it. I arranged for it to be collected the next day.

A few weeks later I needed to visit the store again to buy some rosin, again a warm welcome on entry. My son asked for the rosin for the cello but they only had violin rosin in stock, he was not sure if this would be OK. Tony immediately contacted another store to check, despite having other customers in the shop.

The service I received was superb in every sense and those that know me would say I have very high expectations, especially working in the hospitality industry.

It is important to know that I only spent approximately £5.00 on the book and £2.75 on the rosin.

Tony was polite, attentive, welcoming and most importantly he went out of his way to help me. All the staff members in the shop are excellent and I would not hesitate in recommending this store, not only for all your musical needs but also for a WOW award."

Helen does indeed have very high service expectations. You will be able to read about what her team at Novotel, London West has achieved elsewhere in this book. So well done Tony and to all the team at ABC Music.

It just goes to show that you never really know who you are serving.

First Class Treatment – LEGOLAND

Dawn Stemp has nominated the LEGOLAND staff for The WOW! Awards following her visit. This is what she had to say:

"I am writing to you to draw your attention to the First Class treatment I received from members of the LEGOLAND staff, during my visit.

On arrival at the park, the bus driver dropped me off at the Staff Entrance! Alone, and not knowing where I was, I asked at the security gate how to get into the park. The staff immediately arranged for a young guy to take me by car to the visitor's entrance. I couldn't believe how helpful they all were!

On the short trip to the entrance, I told the driver that I had come to see St Leonard's Mansion, as my Nan had been in service there years ago for the Dodge family. He explained it was now a conference centre and not accessible to the public, but to ask at guest services.

Not holding out a lot of hope, I wondered around the park and can now see why my five year old and eleven year old nephews adore the place! I decided to ask at Guest Services, just in case I could get to see the building. I spoke to a Dutch lady, she was extremely helpful, friendly and even understood my really duff Dutch! A few phone calls later and she had arranged for a car to come and collect me to take me to the mansion. Peter arrived and recognised me from the staff entrance and I pointed out he was my chauffeur for the day!

At the Mansion Ms Lesley Carruthers took me around the building to show me the conference rooms - it really was fantastic! My Nan had told me so many stories of her time in service when I was a child and growing up, now I could see the building for myself. It truly was as if someone had coloured in all the pictures at last! Lesley and the receptionist, Pauline, were both so friendly and welcoming and found time to speak to me and show me around, despite my unannounced trip to the park on the off chance, and their busy work schedules. Visit over, and my 'personal chauffeur', Peter, returned me back to the park itself.

The customer care I receive really was second to none. I left LEGOLAND feeling like a member of royalty!

Please convey my thanks and gratitude to all the staff concerned."

Consider it done, Dawn.

Stairway to WOW! – Attwell Associates, East Sussex

A customer was delighted when a company sent a replacement product free of charge when he bought the wrong one by mistake.

Attwell Associates has won The WOW! Award. This is what customer Phil Brookfield told us about their service:

> "I recently bought a replacement stair spindle from Wickes that was thicker than the damaged spindle it was to replace. Through them I contacted Attwell Associates and a member of their staff very kindly and quickly sent a couple of the 'older style' spindles in the post. All completely free of charge."
>
> Phil sent Nic Attwell a note saying: "Thank you for all your help. It is lovely to get such superb assistance. I have copied this note to a contact who collects and tells stories about good customer service and runs The WOW! Awards. I hope this benefits your business as I am not in the market for any more spindles at the moment!"

We hope that it helps Nic Attwell and his business too, Phil. It's just the sort of service that we're all looking for.

Runaway Success –
Stuart Hale of Performance

There is nothing to beat the personal touch, as this happy customer discovered when the managing director handled her business personally and offered valuable advice

Stuart Hale of Performance went the extra mile for his customer...

A customer called Stuart after seeing an advertisement in a running magazine. When she phoned the business, she was delighted to speak to Stuart himself.

Rather than just taking the order, Stuart took a real interest in his customer's running, training and racing. They had a long conversation in which Stuart offered lots of advice. Stuart also recommended another business that might be able to supply a pair of running shoes.

By going the extra mile Stuart won a raving fan as a customer.

His customer got good advice, and a new friend. In fact Stuart is now her coach.

Going the Extra Mile –
Essex Ford at Basildon

Kate Meager sent me this nomination for Essex Ford at Basildon.

> "We have in the past purchased all of our vehicles from this company as they have always given us great & friendly service. However, recently they (especially Jason) have excelled.
>
> It started when our 18-year-old son on a Saturday afternoon had an accident in his car. It couldn't be driven, we parked it and

phoned Jason at 8 a.m. the following Monday. Initially Jason wasn't really interested in the car - only in how our son was.

By 10 a.m. he had a low loader collect the car and bring it to the garage. Within a few days the repair estimate was with the insurers and Essex Ford arranged a courtesy car for our son until the repairs were complete.

Following this, two weeks later my husband was involved in an accident in our Company Van. This was at 4.30 p.m. on a Friday. In tears I contacted Jason, who again was only interested initially in how Alan my husband was. He then telephoned Alan on his mobile and again arranged a load loader to pick up both the van and Alan. In the meantime, he arranged for us to borrow a demo van to get us through the weekend.

When Alan and the van arrived at Essex Ford, Jason helped transfer all our equipment and 20 sheets of plasterboard onto the loaned van.

Not much credit is given to motor companies. However, Jason and the staff at the body shop at Essex Ford deserve this award. Not only do they give great service but they are also a great bunch of people."

What can I say but, WOW! Well done Jason. And well done Essex Ford.

Bringing Great Service to the Web – Southampton Service Centre

This was the first WOW! Award for an internet business. Hazel Crawford is a regular contributor to The WOW! Awards and sent us this nomination.

"I'd like to recommend someone for your first internet customer service award.

I recently bought a dishwasher but needed an extension fill hose before plumbing it in.

I didn't have any luck finding what I wanted locally, so tried online. The Southampton Service Centre is very helpful and the service is extremely good (especially for a web site). They use a special system, which identifies you by what you want to order, rather than your personal details, so no one else can get hold of them.

They have sent me 3 e-mails confirming my order and asked me to fill in an online feedback form with customer testimonials. You can view other customers' testimonials. I could only find 1 dissenting testimonial, complaining that they had not received their order within a week. I thought you may be interested to see the last email I received from them with the details of the testimonials."

'Hello again,

We are pleased to advise you that the part(s) you ordered are being despatched to you today.

If you are happy with the service you have received from us, (and haven't done this before), would you be kind enough to spare a few minutes to go to our website and fill in the report form to be found by clicking on the "epublic eye" button on the bottom of the homepage? (Don't forget to fill in the 'comments' section, otherwise nothing shows up on the report!)

You, our customer are our most valuable asset, and best advertising agent!

Many thanks again for your business'."

WOW! Great story Hazel. Thank you for the nomination.

Encouraging customers to give feedback has really been put to good use in this case. It's always great to know what customers really think. And, in this case, putting testimonials up for other customers to see is a really brave move. It can only help encourage new customers.

What are you doing to get feedback from your customers?

And once you get it, how do you put it to good use?

Accounting for Good Service – Tom Carroll Associates

This nomination came from Wayne Marshall of Mayet Media Ltd in Warrington. And here's Wayne's story:

Accountants, Tom Carroll Associates, put the WOW! Factor into their customer care. It goes without saying that whilst I was at Tom Carroll Associates I received excellent advice in an easy to understand manner that was concise and jargon-free. That advice saved me a considerable amount of money, but there was another WOW! factor. From the moment I arrived at their office to the moment I left I felt as though they really cared about me, whether or not I was a client.

Just arriving at the office was an experience itself. With the neatly manicured garden and the cheerful entrance it was more like arriving at a theme park than a firm of Chartered Accountants. I had been pre-warned by a colleague who had already sampled the 'Tom Carroll

Experience' to expect an unsurpassed level of service but even so I was still wowed!

The door was answered by an extremely cheerful team member who made me feel at ease straight away. And as soon as I walked in, I saw my name on the (PC) welcome screen. That was really special and made me feel that they were prepared for my visit.

Having been shown into the bright, airy and comfortable conference room, I was given a card that detailed a range of free services that they could carry out for me during my meeting. This included answering my mobile phone or charging it if the battery was running low, even getting traffic information for my onward journey.

There was also a range of catering options that would put many a high street café to shame. During my meeting, when on top of being saved a considerable sum, a plate of hot buttered teacakes was brought, unannounced, to the table. I really was having my cake and eating it!

At the end of the meeting, as I was being escorted back through the reception area, I noticed the umbrellas at the door. 'We use them to escort clients to their cars when it's raining,' said Tom when I enquired. Wow! What a touch.

I know several business people who have experienced the same level of care at Tom Carroll Associates and there is certainly a culture of customer care with a wow. I often recommend people who want to learn about customer care to visit Tom's office and none of them have been disappointed.

This is not the first time that a firm of accountants has been nominated for The WOW! Awards and I don't suppose that it will be the last.

So why is it that accountants seem to be scoring so highly? After all nobody usually associates accountants with service. Or do they?

Well there is a very good reason for it.

Some years ago, a guy called Paul Dunn brought a programme called The Accountants Boot camp to the UK. Paul created a network of accountants around the world who were committed to extraordinary customer service. This network is now known as RAN ONE.

The Boot camp had its disciples, one of whom was Steve Pipe. Steve established another network, also for accountants, called the Added Value Network. And Steve shared Paul's passion for service.

These two networks flourish in the UK with a combined total of around 800 member firms. So I'm not surprised that we've had several winning firms who are accountants. In fact, I'd be surprised if we don't see a few more!

It just goes to show that good service is possible from any business. Just look at the things that Tom Carroll is doing – hot buttered teacakes! It's got nothing to do with accounting but it's got everything to do with delighting customers.

Rolls Royce Standards – The White Hart at Heage, Derbyshire

Angela Wall, from Belper, nominated Malcolm and Marian Hawley for The WOW! Awards after experiencing really great service there.

Angela tells me that:

> "There's always a friendly welcome with attentive service in a clean, pleasant and well-decorated establishment.

You are not hurried, questions are answered well, and all your needs are catered for including the range of food and drinks with lots of options for all types of customers.

The quality of food is exceptionally high - it's well cooked, fresh, quick to arrive, served with a smile and reasonably priced. The ambience is relaxed and inviting - I keep going back for more! And I tell others how good it is. Disabled customers are also well cared for and made welcome. WELL DONE!"

It's a great story Angela.

Everything that you could hope for when going out for a drink or a meal.

It's clear that Malcolm and Marian Hawley have worked really hard to get the service right. Especially since they have only been running The White Hart for 14 months.

You might not be surprised to learn that Malcolm spent 14 years working for the customer service department of Rolls Royce. This just strengthens my belief that the same customer service skills work in any business.

Gita Gould and Jan Carlzon – what a combination!

Back in 1986 I was working for a company that repaired jet engines for the airline industry.

I was finance director and I was just beginning to gather an understanding of the importance of customer service.

One day I heard this quotation that really made me stop and think about first impressions and the way that we handle our customers.

"Coffee stains on the flip tray suggest to the customer that
we do not service our engines properly."

The quotation came from Jan Carlzon who was a past president of Scandinavian Airlines and had rescued that company from financial collapse through his focus on customer service.

Jan wrote a little book called 'Moments of Truth' in which he described his customer service philosophy. This little book was read by thousands of people around the world and became a foundation for customer service delivery.

Gita Gould wins The WOW! Awards for outstanding customer service.

A few weeks ago I was invited to attend a conference at the Runnymede Hotel and Spa at Egham in Surrey.

I arrived rather early and some time before the conference was due to start. Although I was one of the first people to arrive I was warmly greeted by one of the management team at the conference suite, a lady called Gita Gould.

Gita immediately realised that I was early for this event and made every effort to make me feel comfortable. She showed me where the meeting was going to be held and also offered me a range of refreshments and light snacks.

I explained to Gita that I would really like to try and get some breakfast. And so she took me along to the restaurant area. From the very first moment, I really felt that Gita genuinely cared about looking after me. She could so easily have simply pointed me in the direction of the restaurant. But she insisted on escorting me and introducing me to the restaurant manager to be certain that I could enjoy a nice breakfast.

Gita's attention to detail continued throughout the day of the conference and there were a number of instances where I noticed her incredible attention to detail and how much personal attention she gave to each individual.

Nothing was too much trouble for Gita. She had a wonderful warm welcome for all the guests that day. And she literally ran around taking care of everyone.

I noticed how proudly Gita wore a little customer service badge from the hotel alongside the national flag of Denmark on her jacket lapel.

I just couldn't let the opportunity pass without thanking Gita for her superb service. And I felt that, given I was a genuine customer on this occasion, I could nominate Gita for The WOW! Awards.

Yesterday afternoon I went back to the Runnymede Hotel and Spa to present Gita with her certificate from The WOW! Awards.

Gita was genuinely overcome with emotion and gave me a huge hug!

The marketing manager from the hotel, Andrew Duggan, came along to take some photographs. And that's where I thought the story would end.

Gita very kindly asked if I would like some refreshment before continuing on my journey. And the opportunity to enjoy a nice cup of tea seemed too good to miss.

As we stood there chatting, Gita's enthusiasm for her award was undiminished and she kept looking back at the framed certificate that I had given her.

Gita told me that her father would be incredibly proud of her. Her father is now 70 years old and used to be Station Manager at Heathrow airport for Scandinavian Airlines.

"Really!" I said. "Would he have been working for Scandinavian Airlines when Jan Carlzon was president?" I asked.

"Oh yes," replied Gita. "I learnt so much from my father when I was a child."

WOW!
that's what i call service!

Exceeding Expectations – Consistency

How does a business dazzle its customers over and over again? Especially when so much business can come from referrals.

Get it right and people will come flocking to your door.

Let them down and they will be even more disappointed than if they had not heard of you previously.

Consistency is the name of the game in creating true loyalty.

Genuine Care – Barrells Funeral Directors Ltd

Rachel Bridger and her family were certainly impressed when she made this nomination.

My father-in-law died suddenly and we approached Barrells for support.

Colin Barrell came over to listen to us and our stories of our father-in-law - he didn't ask many questions of us - his strength was his ability to listen, empathise and support the ideas that we suggested.

Our father-in-law was well known locally and had a large family so there were many specific things we had to organise including two services - one being at 5pm on a Friday evening and the funeral itself at 2.30pm on a Saturday afternoon - with the burial at about 4pm, when the light was fading fast.

What gave Barrells the 'Wow' for us?

> The way Colin handled the whole process so efficiently with great reverence and yet with great personal touches and a superb eye for detail. He made the funeral a very special day, everyone in the family is still talking about the way his business handled things.

> Little things like - my father in law had a post mortem so we decided that we didn't want to see him again in the coffin as many funeral directors suggest. (My mother in law has had a lot of experience of them through her church role as a verger of services.)

> However two days before the funeral Colin phoned up and said that although we didn't want to see our father in law again - we might like to know that they'd finished making him up and that it 'really is Jim smiling at me' and that 'he looks really great'.

> This encouraged us to see him again - which was a great move by Colin.

After seeing our father in law in hospital just after he had died - he wasn't looking his best - so it was a great relief for his wife and son to see him looking 'restful and calm' again.

Other things that impressed us - the quality of their cars (when the Queen visits Portsmouth she only uses their cars). The way that that the funeral director and his attendants paraded into the village ahead of the car and the way they carried the coffin - level and with great care. The way they sent one of their men ahead to each 'destination' to ensure everything was in place. The way he arranged for roads to be blocked off, with the support of the police, so that our procession had right of way in the village. The way they always bowed when they approached or departed from the coffin. The way they carefully placed the coffin onto a 'dodgy' looking horse and cart that we'd separately organised for the last few hundred yards (our father in law always wanted his final journey to be on a rough looking country cart). The way they offered a lot of support around the graveyard - the way they filled the grave in - it was definitely dark by then.

Sorry to have gone on so much. There is much more I can tell you.... essentially we all went WOW at each stage of the process...and given that we were all pretty shaken up at the time the comfort of having great service was incredibly reassuring and uplifting.

They organised such a great 'weekend' that my young nephews are still talking about it saying 'When can we go to our next funeral it was fun'!

Just reading this nomination again gives me a real sense of how thorough and caring Barrells were. And isn't it interesting how many of the little details were noticed by the family even on such a sad occasion?

Driving Great Service – TC Harrison Ford, Stamford

Filled with dread when you take your car for its MOT? One customer was delighted with the service she got from TC Harrison Ford at Stamford.

This is what Lesley Ann Marston told us in her nomination:

> "At the beginning of June this year the time was fast approaching for my car to have that all-important first MOT; as the car was new in 2000 there's no need for a MOT for three years.
>
> Although I knew the time was nigh I had been very busy and not had time to book the MOT. Then out of the blue a nice lady from TC Harrison called me and politely reminded me that the MOT was due, would I like to book one? This I duly did and I thought afterwards, WOW that's really kind.
>
> About two weeks before the MOT I realised that the 40,000 mile service was also due and thought it would be a good move to get both MOT and service done together. I called TC Harrison and was put through to the Service Dept, whereby a booking was effortlessly made for both.
>
> The morning of the work I was not feeling too well and as the work was likely to take over 3 hours I was faced with the prospect of having to hang around town for that entire time.

Aha, I thought, what about a courtesy car, would they have one free?

At the service desk I was greeted by John Hutchins who was delighted to offer me the use of a car whilst the work was done. So I was happy, I could go home and take it easy.

During the morning I had a call from Darren Allitt in the Service Team. Darren had to break the news to me that although the car would pass the MOT, there were a couple of things that were 'marginal' and needed replacing. He clearly informed me what the cost would be and said that that they could wait, but not for long, if it would be difficult for me to consent to having them done today.

At no time did I feel pressured into making a decision and felt that it was my decision to go ahead and no one else's. WOW - an empowered customer! Darren then said he would call me when Wanda was ready, which he duly did and I set off to collect her.

On arrival at the Service desk I was again greeted by John who had all my paperwork ready and asked me if I was feeling a little better. How nice, I thought, he remembered. Could this Customer Service get any better?

You bet.

John then went through the details of the service, the paperwork, visual health check form etc, and of course that all-important MOT certificate. He explained the work that had been done, and that there was one matter, noted by the

Service Engineer as not needing replacement now but would do so at the next service.

Now came the nasty bit, paying the bill, and predictably, it wasn't a nasty experience at all. John also reminded me about my Nectar points and as I was paying on my Barclaycard I'd get double points. WOW.

From the first telephone call, to collecting my car after the work was done, I felt cared for and cared about, and I won't be taking my car anywhere else!"

With something as complex as a car there seem to be so many opportunities for something to go wrong. It is so refreshing when the situation is handled as nicely and as thoroughly as this one. It's also an excellent reflection on how well the team at TC Harrison Ford work together.

WOW!
that's what i call service!

Going the Extra Mile – Ian Taylor School of Motor Racing, Hampshire

The Ian Taylor School of Motor Racing was nominated for The WOW! Awards by Jon Morter.

"My day there was a present from my wife," said Jon. "Quite frankly, the bunch of people that run the place so smoothly are probably the best example of teamwork and customer relations that I have ever encountered."

And Jon is himself bit of an expert on customer service. He used to work for hi-fi retailer Richer Sounds (this business has been in The Guinness Book of Records every year since 1991 for the highest retail sales per square foot of any retail organisation). In fact, Jon was one of the top employees at Richer Sounds for the customer service that he gave customers.

"Everything about the day was superb.

The Team at the racing school made a special effort to look after my wife and young son whilst I enjoyed myself on the track.

Getting a photograph with one of the cars was no problem – even though it put out their routine and I really liked the way that everyone was so friendly and introduced themselves.

Driving around a racing circuit is a real thrill but what my wife, my son and I remember most is the wonderful friendly service. We all came away with huge beaming smiles after being treated so well."

And if you have any doubts about Jon's enthusiasm as a customer you should know that Jon drove all the way from Southend in Essex to the Hants circuit just to present this certificate; a round trip of 230 miles!

Andrew Franklin is General Manager of the racing school and he was delighted to receive the award. In fact, he gave Jon and I a few laps around the circuit in a Ferrari 360!

Fantastic car, fantastic service! If you're looking for a present for a husband, wife, friend or partner, I can recommend this.

Wedded to Great Customer Service – Newbury Manor Hotel

If there's any one day that great service matters, it's your wedding day. Newbury Manor Hotel WOWED the bride, the groom and all the guests on Jane Hall's wedding day.

"This one comes very much from the heart as it centres round a very special day in my life and that was my wedding day," says Jane Hall, who nominated Newbury Manor Hotel for its great team. Here's what Jane told me:

"My boyfriend proposed back in October of last year, then began the inevitable task of finding a location and venue. All the venues we initially went to see in our area (Hertfordshire) seemed 'tired' or the staff seemed to treat us like any other 'herded' potential bride and groom. We decide to 'surf' further afield and came across the Newbury Manor Hotel's web site (in Berkshire).

From the minute we made contact with the hotel we knew we had come across something very different. The receptionist was very helpful and polite, happy to send a brochure through and encouraging us to pop in anytime for a visit. We decided to see it for ourselves after the brochure arrived and we were very impressed. It is the people that work there, you see, and I always say people are everything. It is apparent that the members of staff love their work, they are very professional, very knowledgeable and they take their roles very seriously and help create a very special environment.

The privately owned hotel is set in beautiful grounds; it has a river running through it, an old water mill, an ideally placed river bar and an award winning restaurant. The key ingredient however for us choosing this venue was the staff.

We decided to organise a date with the wedding coordinator.

We met some great people that first day; Caroline Porter the wedding coordinator, who was chatty, enthusiastic and very personable, Jonathan who plied us with many varieties of wines to sample for the wedding banquet and the River Bar manager, Tom who made sure we had superb service at the River Bar afterwards. In fact every member of staff made us feel extremely welcome and that we were really important to them. My then fiancé turned to me and said this is where he wanted to get married! What could I do but agree.

On the day before the wedding my son, my parents, myself, some other relatives and two of my close friends went down. All the staff took care of us. Our every need was seen to with cheerful dispositions and professionalism, nothing was too much trouble. I met our master of ceremonies, Tom. I was struck how professional, thorough and customer driven he was. Not wishing to pry I asked his age - a mere 17 I was told. How inspiring this young man was, he made me relaxed, focusing on all the things he and his colleagues would be taking care of during our day, reassuring me that all I needed to do was enjoy it.

I went to get ready for dinner that night on a high that all was going so well. I then went down to dinner that evening with family and friends and was again extremely impressed by the restaurant staff like Jonathan, with never ending patience, answering many queries on food, dietary requirements etc. I would also like to mention Marco, who has a fantastic knowledge about cheese and patiently went through each one on the platter - explaining each one in detail. There must have been about 30 of them as well!

What of the day itself you ask? Well it could not have been more magical. Really. All our guests said it was the best wedding they had ever been too. Their comments were that the service was second to none, the wedding banquet was incredible, food is always hard to get right at weddings but this was done with ease. Lastly everyone remarked on how wonderful the staff were. They were all WOWED!

I would like to say a huge heartfelt thank you to the Newbury Manor Hotel for making our day so special and nominate them for a WOW award. Particularly thanks to Caroline and her colleagues, both of the

Toms (River Bar and master of ceremonies), Jonathan and Marco and in fact the entire bar staff and waitresses and waiters who ensured that our day was so special."

Everyone will remember a great wedding. And the association of all the fantastic experiences of that day with the service that was received from Newbury Manor Hotel will live on in people's memories for a long time.

What are you doing to create great memories?

A Piece of Cake! – Lakeland, Guildford

When Paul Georghiou needed bakery supplies, he was impressed with Lakeland's attention to detail.

Paul Georghiou has nominated Lakeland in Guildford for a WOW! Award. This is what he told us:

> "I often go in there to buy baking things for the quite large quantity of home-made cakes that I produce. On this occasion I had bought some loaf tin liners, circular baking parchment for lining cake tins and a couple of other little bits and pieces that I can't easily find anywhere else.
>
> At the till, before the assistant started scanning my purchases, I was asked, 'did you manage to find all the things that you were looking for?'
>
> I had, and told her so but was impressed with the idea of asking the customer. Lakeland sells such a variety of items (like elastic bands and waxed discs for jam jars, baking beans, labels for home made preserves, the list is endless) that quite often, it is impossible to find all you are looking for.

Had I said no, I couldn't find whatever, presumably she would have taken me off to find it. I guess someone has realised that it is difficult to find everything amongst such a large array of items on display and has taken action to ensure everyone purchases everything they came in for.

While the assistant was scanning my purchases, she asked if I had all the latest catalogues. Once again, I had. However, if I hadn't, they would be slipped into the carrier bags for me, with my purchases."

Now this might seem like very simple stuff and not terribly impressive at first glance. But just think it through.

Firstly, if Paul hadn't been able to find exactly what he wanted or didn't have a catalogue, then these simple questions could well have increased the value of Paul's purchase.

A key method of growing any business is to increase the average sales value. But, more importantly, Paul's perception was 'what great service'. And when we get great service that's when we start to become loyal as a customer.

And, of course, another way of growing a business is to get customers coming back more often. It may be very simple stuff but most businesses are not doing it. And they're missing an opportunity.

Customer service is everyone's department – Debenhams, Sheffield

Debenhams wins a WOW! Award for the patience and efficiency of a key team member.

Sometimes customer service is about taking time with the customer to help them with every detail of their shopping decision. Other times, it's about helping them shop as quickly as possible so they can attend to their children or do other shopping. Making sure that important details aren't overlooked when customers are in a hurry is a skill that this WOW! Award winner has achieved.

Customer Peter Entwhistle writes:

> "On Sunday 9 December I was in Debenhams, The Moor, Sheffield, looking to buy a pair of curtains for my living room. (A very big decision as I had forgotten the wall paper samples to match it against.)
>
> A lady called Veronica served me. She was very patient gave very good advice on ready-mades versus made to measure, and saved me £239.00 by advising me to buy the ready-mades. Veronica then took the 4 pairs of curtains out of their packets to match the pattern and check the colours.
>
> It was very busy at the tills as it was a cardholder's special event day. Veronica took my card to the till and re-packed the curtains for me so I didn't have to wait. And she was very insistent that if they did not match when I got them home I could bring them back.
>
> Having two children with me who were very bored, Veronica could see I needed to be out of the shop as quickly as possible after making my decision and did her best to assist me. At all times she was very pleasant and courteous and definitely did more than just sell the goods."

What a great ambassador for Debenhams Veronica is. Peter will certainly be doing his shopping there again and referring his friends.

Short and Sweet – James Hughes, Lloyds TSB, Walton-on-Thames branch.

James Hughes is a cashier and was nominated by Sandra Slight

> "Over the past 6 months, I have found James to be excellent with his customer service skills and without being specific with one experience, it is his CONSISTENCY that I am extremely impressed with. This includes not only his dealings with me, but also my observations of his dealings with other customers.
>
> He makes unprompted efforts to satisfy; he is courteous, friendly and incredibly professional. It is not only these attributes, but importantly, it is his consistent manner and customer service skills that mean I would like to nominate him for a WOW award."

Praise indeed for James from Sandra Slight who is a customer service manager with British Airways.

And James' character shone through when he made his presentation to the judges for the final of The WOW! Award of the year, 2006.

Perhaps having grown up in South Africa and then coming to the UK, James has an extremely refreshing attitude and approach to customer service. On one occasion he even gave a customer some of his own South African rands as she would not otherwise have been able to obtain any foreign currency at very short notice.

I can see that James is a manager of the future for Lloyds TSB. His attitude to leadership, team work and consistency all really impressed the judges.

Starting the year with customer care foremost – New Inn, Clovelly

New Year's Eve can be a frantic time for catering businesses, but one couple was delighted to find the system of the New Inn in Clovelly could cope with their 'fussy' dietary needs.

This is what they told us:

> "My wife and I are vegetarian and on top of that, my wife is allergic to onions, and detests courgettes and aubergines. For this reason we very rarely go out to eat, as almost every vegetarian option has these ingredients. However, for New Year 2001 we thought we would have a change and we booked into the New Inn, in Clovelly, for a two night stay including New Years Eve.
>
> On New Year's Eve there was a six course meal - a scary thought for our fussy eating habits. I warned them beforehand that we were vegetarian and my wife could not eat onions. But being typically British, I didn't want to create too much fuss and explain about the courgettes and aubergines.
>
> When we turned up on New Year's Eve, we were greeted by staff members who were genuinely interested in where we had come from and how the weather had affected our journey. It wasn't the 'thank you for flying with So & So Airways' robotic customer service routine, it was genuine interest. They then produced a detailed vegetarian option menu for the evening starting with Stilton soup and leading on to a number of delicious sounding courses. At this point I thought I ought to advise them about the aubergines and courgettes - this

information was quickly passed to the chef, who advised the menu was all clear.

Later, whilst in our room, we had a very apologetic telephone call to say the soup actually contained a small amount of onion and two alternatives were suggested. Both sounded perfect!

On turning one of the lamps on, I noticed the bulb had blown - it wasn't an important lamp but I reported to reception anyway. Within two minutes of reporting it, a man turned up and repaired the lamp. I hadn't expected that at all - it was 7pm on New Year's Eve in a village that has only just got electricity and someone turns out straight away!

On the second night, the chef came up to us to run through his ideas for the evening meal and to check they were all OK.

We left the New Inn feeling that our fussy issues, which normally would have been seen as a burden, were seen as a nothing out of the ordinary and something that the system is geared up to handle.

Why do I think they deserve a "Wow" Award? Because they treated us like human beings; they handled our diet without a single problem (most places we have eaten before tend to ignore the onion problem by not telling us that something has onion in - going by the theory if it doesn't have onion in the title, then they won't know...) they are geared to provide excellent service even at the most unusual of times and the service went far and away beyond what we expected."

It is often hard to accept that other people have needs which are different to our own. My Mum can never come to terms with the fact that I don't have milk in my tea or potatoes with meat. After more than five years she still tries to give me both these combinations.

It takes special effort to appreciate other people's needs. And the New Inn proved that it can be done and makes a real impact on their customers.

Complete WOW! – The Marriott Hotel, Shipley

There is a risk that some businesses might excel for some customers at the expense of neglecting others. This story shows how a hotel has made exceptional service part of its basic offering.

For consistent service throughout the hotel, The Marriott won a WOW! Award...

Mark Edwards nominated The Marriott Hotel at Shipley for its exceptional service throughout and gave a special mention to the receptionist, conference centre manager and the porter.

"All the participants regarded the overall experience as being outstanding. Everything about the place was so good," says Mark.

The receptionist was friendly and inviting. She helped Mark get some aspirin from the ladies' toilet to treat his cold. The staff in conferencing worked tirelessly to resolve a problem with the presentation equipment he was using. The team in the restaurant was superb. The waitresses did everything that his group could have asked for.

"One other experience was that I kept seeing two men cleaning the corridors," says Mark. "Every time that I saw them they were busy. They said good morning, they opened doors for me. And they kept cleaning and polishing. Everything that could be cleaned was being cleaned."

"We came away from the hotel feeling 'knocked out'. Everyone there took pride in their work and showed outstanding team effort. This story is not spectacular because of any one event. It's amazing because it was so complete and consistent," says Mark.

I made arrangements to visit the Marriott Hotel and present operations manager, Steve Roberts, and his team with The WOW! Awards certificate.

When I arrived, Steve told me how they had recently done some customer service training. And that the word 'wow' was a part of their regular vocabulary. In fact they had had a large sign made up that simply said 'WOW' in great big letters.

Steve had arranged for a local press photographer to come along and record the presentation. Imagine how delighted we were when the photographer asked us all to stand behind this big sign and shout 'WOW!'

WOW! is one of the few words that you can see what people are saying just from the expression on their face.

Very PC – Simon Kaye, Eurosimm

Nominated by Lynda Snowden:

> "I ordered a PDA from Eurosimm. But when it arrived the packaging, through no fault of theirs, had been damaged and I was concerned about the contents.

I contacted Simon via email and expressed my concerns. He immediately replied and informed me that he had passed my email on to the relevant department for them to contact me - I honestly didn't think I would hear anything more.

Imagine my surprise when I then received a telephone call from Eurosimm, expressing their dismay and offering me an immediate discount. I was so taken aback that I forgot to get the caller's name.

I contacted Simon again to thank him for his intervention and to ask him to pass my thanks on to the person who had phoned me.

Within a couple of days I found my computer ignorance was causing problems with my PDA usage. Although I was being cheeky, I contacted Simon to see if he could help. He gave me a fantastic reply (written in basic English for someone such as myself who is not very computer literate) and the problem was solved.

Never knowing when to let a good thing go, I contacted him again with yet another problem. His honesty amazed me. He said that he couldn't help but he gave me all the information he possibly could to point me in the right direction to get help from another source. He even contacted me after that to see if I had achieved any success.

He did far more than he should have done and my instincts tell me that, if I were to contact him in the future, he would be just as helpful. I honestly wish there were more people like him as he actually restored my faith in human nature. I find lethargy and indifference are modern traits and it was so wonderful to be in contact with someone who baulked the trend. I do hope he gets this award as he is a rare individual whose efforts ought to be acknowledged."

Customers certainly do appreciate receiving great service. And Lynda has certainly demonstrated this in her nomination. It's not just a simple 'thank you'. Lynda has taken the time to spell out in detail what happened.

Fine Wine! – Laithwaites

We had several nominations for Laithwaites.

Bill Tyson said:

> "I submit Laithwaites not because of one special event, but because they have consistently provided excellent service. This has been especially demonstrated when problems have occurred and how they have dealt with them e.g. delivery and wine quality issues."

Colin Wright said:

> "I have been a member of Laithwaites Wine Club for three years and in that time I have had impeccable service in terms of quality of goods, speed of service and helpfulness and efficiency at all times.
>
> Unlike all other all centres I have had to contact, Laithwaites are efficient to the point of being unnerving - they have always answered the phone before the first ring has finished. They are remarkably polite and helpful, they know what they are talking about and I have never had even a query let alone a problem.

Promises of delivery dates - given as up to 14 days - I have come to ignore as goods have never taken more than 5 days to arrive.

It was with some surprise therefore that early last month half a consignment had not arrived within 7 days. I telephoned them because (a) it was so unusual and (b) because I needed the ordered goods quite soon for a conference.

Although they were perfectly within their rights to ask me to wait until the 14 days were up they ignored this, quickly checked their records and, although they were able to tell me within a few seconds that the goods had been despatched, they offered to ship another consignment at their cost and at the higher cost of express delivery. They did this I understood because I had told them I needed the goods that week.

Sure enough they arrived the following day. I cannot commend them too highly not just for the quality of their service but also for the cheerful way in which they go about it. It is like dealing with a local shopkeeper you have known for years."

I was only too pleased to nominate them for this award. They truly deserve it."

Tony Bowden said:

"Laithwaites' normal service levels are 1st class; in my case always 100% on time and in full.

They recently introduced a new contact service where they call you, never ever pushy, more like a chat with an old friend about a much loved subject (wine).

On placing an order this way I happened to mention how convenient it was but that I would miss out on any promotional gifts.

A senior member of management rang me back, within an hour, apologised and within 3 days I had received a gift (an espresso coffee service).

Now that's what I call a WOW service!"

Coping with the Seasons – The Cock of the North restaurant, Hertford

To ensure that quality is consistent, companies need to have systems that can maintain standards even when the business is under pressure. No industry is a better example of that than the catering business at Christmas time, which is why Hertford pub The Cock of the North deserves its WOW! Award for providing WOW! against the odds. This is what nominator John Stevens had to say:

"Ten of us went to the Cock of the North for a pre-booked Christmas meal and celebration. And the overall experience was a Wow! Despite the establishment being more than fully booked with large parties and casual diners and drinkers, we were received with exceptional courtesy, kindness and pleasant helpful service.

At no time were we rushed and made to feel as if the table was booked for another party and we should finish as soon as possible. Most of the staff were young but clearly had been handpicked and very well trained by the excellent, pleasant and professional manager. Their cheerful and careful service, level of attentiveness and consideration was exceptional, especially considering their young age.

In addition, the quality of the food was outstanding, given that it was in effect a 'standard fare' Christmas meal. So in all respects the experience was a WOW compared to that normally experienced in UK restaurants and I can, without hesitation, recommend them for an award."

WOW!
that's what i call service!

Recovery

When things go wrong we have a huge opportunity to make amends and win back a customer.

Nobody expects perfection every time.

Great customer service has to be at least conceived by individuals and most often delivered by individuals. And so customers half expect that something may go wrong. But what they really hope for is that there will be systems in place to remedy a problem rather than let it get worse.

Here are some fabulous examples of businesses that get it right even when it goes wrong.

Thank you but no. John Lewis have their own ways of doing things

This nomination was received from Paul and Alice Robinson:

> "Having just returned from a days shopping I must nominate a lady named Sue who works in John Lewis's restaurant at Cheadle for a WOW award.

My wife and I went there for a cup of coffee and snack. Displayed on the menu board was crepe with black cherries, which my wife said she wanted. Sue said. "I am sorry we have sold out but would be delighted to make any other crepe on the menu".

Being a big kid, my wife said she would sulk and stamp her feet (only joking though) as she particularly wanted the black cherry crepe, Sue said she was very sorry and hoped my wife wouldn't sulk too much and continued to serve us with a pot of tea, coffee and a scone. Off we went to find a table.

About 3 minutes later I spotted Sue wandering around the Cafe with a plate in her hand.

She then arrived at our table with a black cherry crepe. They had managed to find a few black cherries and set it down in front of my wife because Sue said she could not have an unhappy customer. And what was even more amazing, she said there was no charge!

This, to me, is service worthy of a mention when you consider the amount spent was less than £5. Sue did not need to go to any further trouble. We were already satisfied customers as the staff and Sue had fully dealt with the lack of black cherry crepe in a fun and friendly way.

So Sue had then gone out of her way to delight the customer and ensure we will certainly recommend John Lewis's to everyone we meet.

In these days where people constantly complain of poor service here was one example of outstanding service worthy of a mention."

Of course, I was delighted to get this story from Paul and Alice. Straight away a letter went off to John Lewis. But the reply we got back was a little unexpected.

Turns out that John Lewis would prefer not to accept The WOW! Award. For them, they have a system of their own for handling customer service excellence. They have simply asked that we pass on the customers' details so that they can thank the customer and Sue in their own way.

Was I disappointed?

Of course. A little.

But in a way, it just made the story even more amazing.

Paul Dean Lewis of British Airways

This particular nomination came from Geoff Perkins and was just one of many commendations and testimonials from customers received about Paul.

> "Following a recent and fairly traumatic personal situation my wife suffered an unprecedented panic attack prior to boarding our flight to Barbados.
>
> The attack was so severe that she had to be driven by buggy to the lounge and then onto the gate. Even at the gate it was touch and go as to whether she would make it onto the aircraft.
>
> Once on board (after some help from the captain) Paul took over and provided a one to one service from push back, through take off and initial climb. He provided re-assurance

and genuine concern and my wife was much calmer as a result.

It has to be said that all the BA staff on this occasion were excellent; from check in, to the lounge and the gate staff who arranged for the captain to come out of the flight deck to speak to my wife.

However, Paul went the 'extra mile' and turned what could have been a very difficult experience into one that was memorable for the right reasons."

This story reminds me that we don't deal with businesses. We only ever deal with people who represent businesses. The reputation of a huge company rests on thousands of individuals doing the right things on millions of occasions.

Everyone working to WOW! – De Vere Belton Woods Hotel

The De Vere Belton Woods Hotel has certainly empowered its team to deliver WOW wherever it's needed...

This is what Mark Gee had to say in the nomination:

"I have stayed in many hotels in the UK and abroad including some of the most expensive but have rarely seen such excellent customer service. During our stay every person connected to the hotel that we came in contact with gave us the same high standard of customer care, from the housekeeping staff right through to the management.

"Whilst in some expensive hotels the service can seem to be forced, I found that everyone within the hotel seemed to have a genuine belief in finding ways to please their guests. Nothing was too much trouble and all staff seemed to be empowered to ensure that they deliver the excellent service required.

"To give some examples: When we arrived in our room we found that the fridge had not been connected and we informed reception. Within minutes we were visited by someone from housekeeping who explained that the fridges were new and that they were being connected by the hotel's electricians during the next few days. We explained that having a baby meant that we would need a fridge and the housekeeper offered to try to get the fridge connected and if not let us use the main fridges in the hotel with 24 hour access. Less than half an hour later we were visited by the electrician who duly ensured that we had a working fridge available.

"I overheard a conversation between a young member of staff in one of the bars and some guests. It was evident that the guests had ordered a sweet that was now not available and were being offered an alternative. The alternative would be more expensive and the guests asked whether they would have to pay extra to which the reply was, "no it is our fault that we have run out, not yours, so please choose whatever you want for no extra charge". What was impressive about this was that the member of staff could take responsibility for this decision without having to 'go and check'.

These two are just some of the examples I came across in what was only a two day stay, which left me with a general feeling of superb service and a real 'can do' attitude from the whole Hotel team."

Isn't it great to be dealing with employees who are truly empowered? One of my greatest frustrations is people who cannot handle a complaint. If ever I hear the words, "What you need to do is…" or "If you can just…" I know that I'm about to be disappointed.

In my own business we created two little systems.

The first was called "Complain Right". This was our system for handling complaints. It's much better to write down and communicate what you expect your people to do if a customer complains.

The second system was called "Dazzle Right". This set out exactly how much authority every single member of our team had to resolve a complaint.

What are your systems?

Maxi Service from a Mini Garage – Synter Mini, West Midlands

Garages often get a bad press, but a customer was delighted with the service delivered by Synter Mini.

Synter Mini in the West Midlands has won a WOW! Award for its after-sales care. Here's what customer John Price who nominated the business told us:

> "I bought a new Mini Cooper from Syntner in April and had been impressed by the service that I had been given not only by the sales staff but also the after sales team.
>
> On the 17th May (Friday) I suffered a puncture. This was particularly galling, as the car has run flat tyres and they

cannot be repaired and the car had only done 1300 miles - effectively a brand new tyre!

Additionally, there is no spare as the tyres are still effective even when punctured. However on the Saturday I was due to visit my brother in Haverhill, Suffolk a journey of some 130 miles and I needed to get the tyre replaced.

My initial call to the garage directed me to ATS/KwikFit etc., as their tyre fitter did not work on a Saturday. I was beginning to have misgivings about the run flat tyres and lack of spare wheel. I phoned all my local suppliers - they could get me a tyre for Monday - this was useless to me a) because I needed to make the journey to Suffolk and b) I was going away on holiday on the Monday.

I called the garage back and enquired if I could buy a tyre from them and take it to a tyre fitter to be fitted. The service receptionist asked me to bear with him whilst he made some enquiries - he would phone me back.

Within 10 minutes he had phoned me back to say that he had arranged with their own tyre fitter to come into the garage and could I get there within the next half hour so they could sort out my problem.

I was absolutely delighted. They had removed the burden of worry from me. The tyre was duly fitted and the car returned to me washed and the interior vacuumed out.

Garages often receive bad press but I have nothing but praise for the professional, courteous and helpful manner with which I am cared for by Sytner Mini."

Now that is impressive.

John is exactly right. "They removed the burden of worry".

That would make a really great objective for any business to think about.

Sparkling Service – Jewell Fleet Services, Osyth

This WOW! winner helped a customer out of a tricky situation and asked for nothing in return.

Mike Faulkner made this nomination for Jewell Fleet Services, Pump Hill, Osyth. He says:

> "On a journey out of London four weeks ago, one of our passengers was taken suddenly ill, and had the misfortune of vomiting all over the inside of the passenger door, floor and seat.
>
> Having taken the passenger safely home and cleaned as much of the car as possible, I was left with the dilemma of how to get rid of the stench. It was not a simple case of valeting the car, as the offending vomit had penetrated between the window and the inside of the door. What valeting company would remove the door panel? What garage would clean vomit from a car? The solution was not a simple one.
>
> I phoned JFS to see whether they knew of a valeting company who would be willing to do the necessary. After empathising with me about the dilemma and asking about the welfare of the patient, they asked if I could live with it for another 48

hours. I said I could as I had access to another vehicle. They then said to take the car to them and they would see what they could do - they promised to improve the situation by 99 percent.

After 24 hours I decided to deliver the car to JFS and leave it there overnight. This was at 1.30pm on Tuesday. At 5.30pm they called and asked me to come and remove the vehicle, I suspected it was overcrowding their forecourt.

When I got there, the car was shining like a new penny. They had valeted the outside, the inside, removed the door panel and steam cleaned inside the door. At that I thought WOW!

As I approached the forecourt, the JFS Manager approached and gave my partner the key, knowing it was her car and it would have to be to her standards. Then Michael, who sold us the vehicle, came and asked how we were, and were we happy with the result? And to complete the picture, the manager of the valeting company came over and said that if the smell came back to let them know and they would valet it again. I asked the manager how much I owed him. He put out his hand to shake mine, and said 'you have suffered enough with this, there is no charge'. I've never known service like that in my life!"

To the Rescue – WH Smith Cheltenham

Spencer Mead has nominated his local WH Smith store and staff for a WOW! Award and this is what he told us:

"I am nominating the store because I am a disabled person in a wheelchair and the staff in my local store will do anything to assist me.

151

On two occasions there has been a power cut in the store.

Rather than leave me to wait for the fire brigade to get me down the stairs from the first floor, three members of staff carried me in my chair (which is an electric chair and is very heavy) down the stairs even though I did warn them that they could injure themselves by doing it.

But they still went ahead and made sure I was safely downstairs and out of the building."

Beyond the Call of Duty – Dee Cee Upholstery Southampton

Andrew Waldron sent this letter to Mr Kaplan of Dee Cee Upholstery and nominated them for The WOW! Awards:

Dear Mr Kaplan.

Thank you so much for the extraordinary help you gave me earlier today, well above and beyond the call of duty!

Through no fault of anyone's but mine perhaps, once I'd spent a couple of days using my new chair I realised that it was not as comfortable as I'd remembered from the brief taste of your showroom demonstrator. This in turn made me begin to imagine that I'd made a serious error in choosing this type of chair at all.

Thanks to your immediate efforts to correct the problem by strengthening some straps and reinforcing the padding, the 'feel' of the chair has been transformed and I'm now, with much relief, appreciating its comforts. Thanks to you my dodgy back is now beginning to recover from the ravages caused by my old chair!

I am utterly certain that the dedicated trouble you took, as well as the skill you demonstrated in working out how to modify my chair to suit my needs, would not have been available had I bought from any furniture chain store. Needless to say I will be recommending you to anyone that I can.

Yours sincerely

Andrew Waldron

Small businesses often find it difficult to compete with the big stores. And so it is even more important to put the emphasis on the service and pay attention to the details.

Andrew clearly appreciated what was done for him and I'm sure that he will be recommending Dee Cee Upholstery to many other people.

Prompt Response – Eurosimm Strikes Again!

Eurosimm have been nominated for the second time running for a WOW! Award.

Nominated by Chris Russon:

"Six months or so ago I purchased an mp3 player from Eurosimm. The price was very good but it was still an expensive purchase, and I felt I was taking a risk buying over the internet.

Recently it seemed to have a developed a fault. I contacted Eurosimm fully expecting a major hassle about the guarantee, exchange, etc. Within a couple of days a courier had arrived to collect the unit, the next day it was confirmed that the unit was faulty, and the brand new replacement arrived by courier a few days after that.

So, customer service that most high street stores could not have matched. Special thanks to Alain for being an excellent communicator and for oiling the wheels of the process throughout."

It's a shame that customers feel so wary about dealing with a new supplier. And when a fault develops, they often fear the worst and are expecting bad service. This gives those companies who are geared up to respond properly an even better opportunity to dazzle and delight their customers.

Chris Made the Difference –
The Hinton Oak Restaurant

Chris the general manager of The Hinton Oak Restaurant has been nominated by Colin Marvell for the way he handled one of the most fractious things in the world: hungry children, especially ones called Amy, Ashleigh and Owen!

"Having had a long day out, it was approaching 5.30pm when we pulled into the Hinton Oak car park, remembering a pleasant family pub who did a good kids menu (a couple of years back).

Somehow it looked different, so Dad was despatched to investigate both restaurant and food.

The pub had been transformed from its homely feel to a very modern, contemporary restaurant, devoid of kids menu.

I put my dilemma (ravenous kids, not open till 6pm, no kids menu) to the General Manager, Chris.

He immediately replied 'No problem, bring them in, they can have anything off of either (lunchtime/evening) menu or we can do them…" and he listed a familiar range of children's fare.

Having decided to stay, Chris then engaged the kids and amongst other things asked them where they'd like to sit and proceeded to help them to choose a table.

Every family has a fussy eater and ours is 8 years old.

Chris took their orders and disappointed our 8 year-old by telling her there were no peas in his posh restaurant, to go with her staple diet of sausage and mash.

On seeing the look on her face he proceeded to go to his flat, upstairs to see what he had in his own cupboards!

Returning, he reeled off a list of options and the spaghetti hoops were unanimously voted for by all concerned.

Chris then ensured that we all had an excellent meal, especially the kids, by engaging them regularly.

We left, vowing to return and thanking Chris for a memorable time. In reply he added modestly 'Don't thank me, it was a team effort'

That may have been the case but the family and I (especially one very impressed 8-year-old) knew we had just been 'Wowed' by Chris himself, who deserved some recognition."

It would have been so easy for Chris to say, 'We are not open until 6 p.m.' or 'we don't have a kids menu'. Colin and his family might still have waited for opening time and then selected something from the menu. They may even have left feeling quite satisfied. But what Chris did by taking this problem on was really quite exceptional.

It's this type of service that The WOW! Awards especially likes to recognise. This is more like treating customers as friends rather than just a source of income.

You can bank on us! Allied Irish Bank, Uxbridge

In the early years of our company, in fact before we became Arora International, owning three large hotels, we chose to bank with Allied Irish Bank because of the amazing customer care we received from our then Branch Manager, Tom Potter.

Tom always treated each of his customers as individuals, giving them an extraordinary amount of his time during and even outside of work hours.

Each time Tom received a promotion, we changed branches of bank because we felt comfortable in the knowledge that he was looking after us. Now the Senior Banking Manager of their Head Office Bank in Uxbridge, Tom still has that personal touch and his team clearly follows his lead as we can expect the same degree of courtesy from anyone that comes into contact with us. Any business acquaintances that we recommend to use their services have nothing but praise for the bank and Tom in particular.

The reason I wish to nominate the Bank for a WOW Award is a result of their going above and beyond the call of duty last November.

We were due to run our payroll at 2pm one afternoon. As we started to process the data, the modem in the PC we have to use went wrong. With only two hours before the BACs office in Belfast was due to close, we were in trouble.

> I placed a call to the Bank in Uxbridge and was transferred to their IT department who immediately took control.
>
> Within 30 minutes, their Linda McCready was at our accounts office in Heathrow with her laptop computer.
>
> Because there would be a delay whilst our data was transferred to her PC, she rang the main office in Belfast and instructed that no one was to go home until the Arora payroll had been run.

This duly happened and 200 or more staff received their pay on time.

I would ask, 'how many other banks would have taken this extraordinary approach and gone so far out of their way to assist a customer in trouble?'

This is why we bank with AIB and will continue to do so. Tom and his team are a wonderful example of WOWing their customers and I hope you will strongly consider them for your prestigious award.

It's a pleasure to recognise Tom and his team at Allied Irish for their outstanding efforts. And it just goes to prove that people choose to deal with people. Not companies!

WOW!
that's what i call service!

Fulfilling the promise

Just look at all the adverts on the television, in the papers and even by the roadside. They all promise incredible things and ultimate satisfaction.

But how many businesses really deliver on those promises?

Here are some that do.

The ultimate WOW! Award for perfect service

How does the biggest organisation in the world organise such perfect service?

And why should one individual from that global organisation be singled out?

When I received this nomination I was fascinated and curious. I decided to do some research (including some mystery shopping and working in this business) before bringing you this story.

Great service is simply a combination of lots of little things. Remember Jan Carlzon (former President of Scandinavian Airlines) – "You cannot improve one thing by 1000% but you can improve 1000 little things by 1%". This organisation follows that rule exactly. Every year they reconsider EVERY aspect of their service delivery and adjust to meet their customer's needs. They take account of age, location and every possible need.

This organisation has fantastic systems. Their systems for order taking and delivery are second to none.

Every single person in this business is motivated by the single most important factor – customer satisfaction. Money simply does not come into it. In fact, some of the people working there are struggling for money – often living below the 'breadline' but still they deliver great service.

I could not believe the training systems that are in place. Successive generations of employees pass on the skills and the customer understanding. These people could each achieve a degree in customer psychology – such is their depth of understanding.

In terms of 'out of the box' thinking, this organisation is incredible. Every aspect of the delivery process is re-engineered each year. Employees and distributors form small working parties to brainstorm and plan how they can do it better.

Communication throughout the organisation is the best that I've ever seen. Communication with customers is done with thought and care. No jargon. No small print. Just pure, simple communication.

They have feedback systems to beat all others. When something is not completely right for the customer, they pay complete attention. They never argue with their customer. They never question if the customer is right. You can see that even the tiniest failure really hurts and is taken very personally. Every mistake is treated as a learning experience and noted for the next time that customer is served.

This organisation has the ultimate guarantee – it never disappoints its customers. In fact, from what I've seen, the relationship between the business and its customers is so strong that customers don't even complain. Everyone accepts that every Team member has done the very best that they could.

Every dimension of care is present in this business. There is huge care and respect for the external customers and for the internal customers. And employees are also encouraged to look after themselves – it's the perfect system.

I have never seen leadership like this before. The vision of how the business should operate is so strong that every employee follows it exactly and without question. Deadlines are set and met every single time without fail. 'Incremental effort' is an expression that these Team members would not understand because they always give their best, sometimes at personal cost to themselves.

The customer is most certainly King in this business. But that's probably because every one of those customers will one day work in the business themselves. It's also because these customers are children and the basics of customer service are learnt when we are children.

The winner of The WOW! Award goes under a variety of job titles according to local customs and traditions. Father Christmas, Santa Claus and St Nicholas are some of the titles that are familiar to me. You may have your own title for this customer service expert.

If only every person in every business took it this seriously.

Happy Christmas!

The stamp of great service from the Post Office, Stevenage

Steve Bachelor was Chairman of Baldock Round Table when he nominated The Royal Mail Sorting Office at Stevenage for The WOW! Awards. Here's the story:-

> "On the day of their ladies night, Colin (the treasurer) had to get £550 in cash from the bank to pay the band.
>
> Colin got the money from the bank; put it in an envelope with an elastic band round it and "£550" written on the side. But it got mixed up with some other envelopes and it ended up getting posted.
>
> At 6.50 PM Colin realised his mistake and rang the sorting office at Stevenage. He spoke to Geoff Fox, Processing Manager, who offered to call back if they found it.
>
> A few minutes later the telephone rings to say that they had the envelope and Colin could collect it. When Colin got to the sorting office he was absolutely delighted and told Geoff so.
>
> "Just doing my job mate," was Geoff's modest reply.

I just love it when I get nominations like this one. The Royal Mail often receives criticism from the media. But let's not forget that any business is made up of people. And most people are doing the best that they can with the resources that they have available.

A Solicitor that Really Cares – Stephen Adshead

Jane Barnes wrote:

Dear Derek,

I am thrilled to be writing to you to make a worthy nomination for The WOW! Awards.

No court case is easy and appears to have an unwritten "do not discuss" at any stage or outcome. However in view of the amazing way I have been treated, I felt that someone, somewhere should be taking notice and I thought of you and The WOW! Awards™!!

Stephen Adshead took over a legal case for me at extremely short notice. He put in a lot of hard work and long hours as well as keeping me informed with advice and help on a number of issues. This was a particularly difficult case and caused me extreme stress while the other side deliberately caused unnecessary delays.

I wish to nominate Mr Stephen Adshead for The WOW! Awards™ - for the best in customer service for his outstanding customer service to me. His service went over and above my expectations and far exceeded any expected contribution from a legal representative, throughout an extremely traumatic legal case.

Stephen not only provided excellent guidance and invaluable support. But when the going got really tough with cross questioning over a two day period, he kept in touch with me after full days at court, updating information, supporting me all the time. And he also told me funny stories at break times regarding the antics of his son, who was just learning to crawl - with hilarious results, to take my mind off the ensuing case and to keep my chin up with regards to the cross examination. WOW!

I wish to say a huge thank you to Stephen for his continued efforts on my behalf throughout the case and for the care and consideration shown by him, which cannot be taught or purchased, because it comes from within and caring about others.

If this is a reflection of the calibre of people at the FRU, then I would recommend that any legal requirements - personal or company orientated - would only benefit from utilising their services.

I DO hope he is successful and will be allowed to accept this award in recognition of his superb contribution in providing outstanding customer service, (coupled with his legal expertise), which will be an excellent benchmark for his employer as well.

Thank you for your consideration.

Kind regards
Yours sincerely

Jane Barnes

Jane's story had that element of WOW! to it that made me feel this was worthy of The WOW! Awards. And so I arranged to go, with Jane, to present Stephen with his certificate.

Stephen has recently joined a new firm, Dawsons Solicitors, and we visited him at his London offices. And there were three further WOW! moments that came out of that presentation.

Firstly, Stephen's wife and, now famous, son had come along to see him receive his certificate. They too were clearly thrilled that Stephen had been nominated for The WOW! Awards.

Secondly, Jane Barnes had turned up with a film crew to record the presentation. WOW!

And third, as I chatted with Stephen about the work that he had done for Jane there were several mentions of the FRU. I didn't wish to appear ignorant and assumed that FRU must be some sort of legal term. But eventually I did ask what FRU is.

It turns out that FRU is the Free Representation Unit. All of Stephen's work for Jane had been done free of charge!

WOW!

Gentle Dental from Newquay in Cornwall.

This is what Jane Ninnes had to say about the special care that she received.

> "I was terrified of dentists as I was needle phobic.
>
> But, through patience and encouragement from Adam, I had my first treatment involving a needle today.
>
> Fantastic service.
>
> Fantastic receptionists.

And, although a private business, not too expensive.

I cannot praise enough."

Well done to Adam Randall and his Team at Gentle Dental.

It's easy to underestimate how difficult it can be for people to visit a place that they have a real phobia of. Adam clearly went out of his way to help Jane.

But it's not just dentists who need to consider their patient's feelings. Many people may feel intimidated or apprehensive about visiting their bank manager, their accountant, a solicitor or anyone who they feel is in a position of authority.

However, if you look at your business through your customers' eyes then the solution should be fairly straightforward.

Lifetime Relationships – Coloplast

Coloplast, a healthcare company operating from Peterborough in the UK, have a great record in the National Customer Service Awards with two wins in recent years and several final places. They have also won several local and regional service and business awards and hold the British Standards Institute ISO 9001 Quality Award.

They work primarily in the highly sensitive customer care arena of providing ostomy care and continence care products and do so to an extremely high standard.

Just look at their record. They succeed in delivering 100% of orders within 48 hours and they do so to 99% accuracy. Each year they receive thousands of thank you letters and Christmas cards, family photos and small gifts from grateful customers. The customers are expressing their appreciation for the fantastic help that they receive from the company in supplying them with very personal medical dressings in a hassle free and sympathetic manner.

The company traces its history to Denmark in the 1950s when Nurse Elise Sorensen, trying to nurse her sister, invented what we would know today as a colostomy bag for human waste management.

Today the company operates in 28 different countries with a significant sales and distribution operation in the UK. The UK team maintain the international company's worldwide reputation for outstanding service and their results show an almost utopian situation but it was not always like this and just four or five years back they were overwhelmed with volume and regularly pulled back by the resulting mistakes and shortcomings.

The simple but well planned and executed recovery strategy serves as a textbook example to any organisation facing a similar situation.

At Coloplast the service normally starts when a hospital patient, having undergone surgery that results in a need for one or other of the company's products, is discharged with a small supply of the product to cover the first week or so. At this stage the customer is generally still coming to terms with the new situation and maybe even considering whether life will be worth living in the future.

Coloplast make a welcome call seven days after the hospital discharge. That first call is very sensitive and personal and calls for a customer care professional able to totally empathise with the customer. The purpose of the call is to enquire how the customer is coping with the sample product provided, ascertain the need and explain the ordering process to the customer.

The company aim to establish a rapport and understanding with the customer so that the customer will remain with them for as long as they continue to need the medical product provided. For most customers this will be for the remainder of their life. So they are very much in the business of building long-term relationships.

The mission for the customer care team is fourfold:

1. Contribute to the quality of life

2. Become close to the customers, understand them as individuals

3. Have a passion for the business of providing care and solutions for the customer

4. Increase value to customers and stakeholders

The key to the quality of their service delivery lies in their home delivery service. Currently they deliver to 300,000 customers on a regular basis, maintaining their fast turnaround and accurate service.

Following the first welcome call, subsequent calls will be undertaken by Coloplast on a regular pro-active basis. By instigating the subsequent calls, the company is saving the customer the trouble and ensuring that the re-order cannot be forgotten, a happening that could result in considerable distress for the customer. From the company's viewpoint they can make sure the call is made, the business secured and that it is all done in good time to make sure that the customer has continuity of supply at all times. Additionally the company can undertake the calls during the less busy times for incoming calls, thus maximising efficient use of staff availability and minimising call waiting.

During the regular calls the customer care team member can continue to build the relationship, check that all is well and plan for special situations such as holidays which may amend the normal order and distribution arrangements.

As to be expected the company has a number of customer care standards against which performance can be assessed. These and the success rates are set out below:

1. **Excellent service – personal and caring.** Every team member has an objective of delighting each customer and building the relationship. Their success can be measured by over 3,000 cards; letters and gifts sent every year as a "thank you" for the service. Incidentally their policy is to recruit customer care staff from "people who have lived and understand a little about life".

2. **Abandon calls.** Currently they run at half the acceptable target of 2% abandoned calls and they also operate a 24-hour internet-dedicated response as back up. In encouraging the team to be mindful of outstanding calls, they are asked to imagine the call waiting number shown on the indicator board as a queue of people standing in front of them waiting to be served. If they were standing in front of you, the argument goes, you would not attend to small jobs that can wait until later but attend to the next customer and do the other things later when the queue has eased.

3. **Delivery standard.** Their delivery standards have already been touched upon. They aim for 100% delivery within 48 hours and they consistently achieve this without fail

4. **Quality and presentation of products.** Against a target of 98% "right first time" order fulfilment, they actually achieve

99% and any failures are turned around immediately. All the warehouse and delivery team members have sat in on the telephone calls, so they have knowledge of what a late or incorrect delivery can mean for a customer.

5. **Prescription debt.** Coloplast is, of course, a commercial organisation and needs to get paid for its work. Payment comes from prescription fees from the National Health Service and it is important that correct details are taken to secure payment. Their target is a prescription debt of no more than 5% and they achieve an even better 3%.

It was not always like this however and they had to re-engineer their processes a few years ago to keep on top of the work to provide an efficient service, reduce errors and reduce the prescription debt.

They undertook a gradual but thorough and methodical review of all their processes. What the company does is basically simple – they take orders for their products, process those orders and then deliver the products. Like many businesses there are a myriad of details that can complicate the processes but essentially the business is relatively straightforward.

The start of their journey to service excellence began with reviewing all the tasks, the volumes and the work cycles. The work cycle review revealed their busy times – early morning and their busy days – Mondays and Fridays. This immediately enabled them to plan their work better and led to the decision to make pro-active order calls. This in turn reduced the abandon call rate (running at 16% in peak times) spread the workload and reduced errors.

The next stage was to discover average unit times for all of their processes. This gave them very powerful information for staffing levels.

Following this they looked into all the required competencies for the customer care team. They produced a skill matrix and asked all members to rate themselves against all of the competencies identified as being needed in the department. This immediately revealed skill shortages and this led to a training plan, individual performance targets, increase in multi-skilling and succession planning.

Prior to this initiative they frequently had situations where some staff members were under tremendous pressure to rise above the workload, whilst other staff members without the skills to assist, were relatively underemployed in their own roles. Now the loads can be shared equally so that no one is overstretched and the customers receive a fast accurate service.

As they began to document all the processes in great detail, they realised that some seemingly simple tasks took a long time to process and they were able to investigate reducing this time by simplifying the process. This often involved liaison with other departments such as distribution, logistics and marketing and led to a greater appreciation all round of the impact that one department's actions can have upon others.

The result of this work also enabled them to understand much earlier the benefits of any proposed changes and from removing any non-value added processes.

All of this resulted in the very high customer care performance that we see today. Their journey has not finished however. They see their quest for excellence is ongoing. They regularly take people out of their roles for a week and ask them to look at a particular process to examine and improve it.

At Coloplast relationships are long standing. They provide outstanding employment conditions to encourage longevity of service. They do not see the kind of turnover associated with most contact centres.

Equally customer relationships are also long standing. They even arrange open days for customers to visit the offices and warehouse and meet the staff to witness the friendliness, efficiency and cleanliness of the operation.

One of the initiatives that best demonstrates the affinity between the company and its customers is the exhibition of artwork submitted by customers and displayed at the offices. The stunning show underlines the fact that whilst customers may have survived a life changing health issue, they are still out there living their very full and active lives.

Some of the reasons why this is so are due to the care; understanding and efficiency of the Coloplast award-winning customer care team. What greater reward can there be?

Sounds Good in America – Thame Audio

Thame Audio's long distance assistance sparked a nomination from abroad.

Buying presents for friends abroad is extremely difficult without the help of a WOW! shop like Thame Audio.

Thame Audio has been awarded a WOW! Award for its outstanding service helping a customer in the US get a present to a friend in the UK. We received this nomination:

> "My friends in Thame bought their son a Surround Sound Receiver for his birthday but no speakers. When I heard of

this I offered to buy a pair of speakers for their son, to go along with the receiver.

I am in New York, they are in Thame, and the birthday was only a few days away. I immediately called the website of the world's largest volume dealer of stereo components located in the UK. Unfortunately they could not accept my credit card order and ship the goods to Thame. So I could not make the deal with them.

I contacted Thame Audio. In the past, I've bought small parts from there and brought them back to my home in New York. The owner of the store was on holiday and his associate Steve was minding the shop. Steve had never heard of me and I explained the situation, that I wanted a pair of speakers as a gift for a friend in Thame.

Steve took my credit card details over the phone and ordered the speakers, which he said he could have there by Friday (the birthday date). Steve even called my friends parents 'discreetly' when the speakers came in.

My friend's son got his speakers on his birthday and was thrilled.

Steve did a great job of getting the exact items I wanted in a short amount of time, with me calling in the order from New York. Now, I can't wait to come back to the UK on holiday and hear my friend's new stereo & speakers."

This nomination from Bob was one of the very first nominations that we received from an American visitor to the United Kingdom. And I was absolutely thrilled to think that we were at last beginning to impress our visitors from overseas. That's what The WOW! Awards is all about.

A Vegetarian Feast – Beefeater, Stanborough

It's easy to be consistent with products that have the greatest demand, but the Stanborough Beefeater wowed a customer with its vegetarian salad and its service delivering it.

Phil Lenton wrote to us to nominate the Stanborough Beefeater. This is what he said:

> "We wanted to take friends out for a meal locally but one wanted a vegetarian salad without it being too ordinary. I felt that I should check that my choice of venue, a particularly nice country pub, would be flexible in its catering. But they were unable to offer very much.
>
> The second choice could not accommodate us this evening so I tried the Stanborough Beefeater. The person I spoke to on the phone was very helpful and promised to take note of the needs of my friend. She told me her name was Jenny and suggested I ask for her if I needed help when we arrived. In the event we were served by another, equally helpful, waitress called Sarah. Not only was the meal excellent but the waitress who I'd spoken to on the phone did stop at our table and engage us in conversation.
>
> Because of the flexibility and the excellent service that we received we are now regular visitors to this restaurant. The Team deserves The WOW! Award."

Pursuit of Excellence – Yorkshire Bank

When Pete Snowden was declared the Customer Service Professional of the Year in the second year of the National Customer Service Awards, he protested that he did not think that he was the best customer service professional in the country but that he was happy to accept the award on behalf of the team at Yorkshire Building Society.

As a result of his comments, the majority of the award classifications, including that of the overall winner, were amended to reflect team rather than individual success. However nothing detracts from the great efforts made by Pete in helping to transform the Yorkshire from a rather staid, product driven organisation into the customer focused company that we see today.

With over thirty years service with the Yorkshire, Peter has primarily served in operational roles and has always put the customer at the heart of what he does.

Some years ago, he was invited to apply for the somewhat quaintly titled position of Member Relations Manager. This was, he explains, a fancy title for Complaints Manager as the company did not want a title that admitted that it received complaints from time to time. He stated at the interview that he would accept the job only if the position could be expanded to encompass a wider service remit rather than just focusing on complaints. He explained that he saw the future prosperity of the company depending upon the quality of service, as there was very little in terms of product differentiation to separate the various financial institutions with whom they competed.

Somewhat to his surprise, his terms were accepted and he set about building great customer relations based upon listening to customers and providing the staff with the tools to do their job. Until his appointment, it was probably true to say that, not unlike most comparable organisations at the time, the company never really listened to their customers.

It was true that each month they sent out a questionnaire asking how satisfied with the service the customers were and these came back regularly reporting a satisfaction rate of around 89% and that kept everyone happy. Any comments added to the questionnaire were largely ignored because there was no way that these could be recorded on the system being used.

Pete, encouraged by senior management, set about changing perceptions. He put pursuit of service excellence at the top of the agenda. He used the word pursuit intentionally as he felt that service excellence is a journey rather than an arrival as the bar is continually being raised and significant improvements lead naturally to increased expectations.

His definition of service excellence was "everything we do to win, retain and delight profitable customers and when we fail, we recover brilliantly".

One of his early initiatives was the setting up of a 4000 strong research panel of customers drawn from across the spectrum, who could be consulted across the board or in small groups on various issues affecting them and the society.

Customer drivers (New customers versus existing customers)

He quickly learnt that existing customers have different drivers to stay with an organisation than new customers. Whereas new customers are attracted by price, image and size, existing customers stated their rather different needs rather more precisely. They wanted reliability, to be treated as individuals, ease of doing business and as little hassle as possible, especially when things go wrong and mistakes happen.

Pete realised that in some respects customers were asking for a return of the 'good old days' that ended somewhere at the end of the 1980s. Until then the business had been conducted on a localised basis where staff pretty much knew the names and details of all the customers. Then, in keeping with rival organisations, the Society began to shave costs in order to remain competitive.

Although they managed to improve cost efficiency and grow the business, something was lost in terms of personal service and Pete's mission was to restore the service without increasing the cost base.

A fair bit of his work was centred on the view as to what it was that makes the Yorkshire different. This was defined in terms of Purpose, Virtues and Vision as under:

Purpose: To maximise long term benefits for a growing membership

Virtues: Fairness, fun, passion, people working together

Vision: Famous for being recommended

From this devolved the values statement, which – importantly for Pete – was not just to be a printed statement pinned on the wall and forgotten. Every group within the Society draws up an action plan as to how they are going to work to the values and to make sure that the action plans are not just pinned up alongside the values statement and similarly forgotten, every so often the values are revisited and the process starts again.

Even today, Pete confesses that he does not know if the Yorkshire can be described as "famous" for being recommended but it is a fact that 40% of new business comes from member recommendations.

The member panels have been a tremendous catalyst for service improvement at the Society. Having worked with the member panels for some time, Pete has become more committed than ever in his belief that involving customers in decisions is the key to providing not just customer satisfaction but true customer advocacy.

Customer satisfaction surveys are still carried out but today all comments are given serious consideration and they also meet with customers at regular road shows. As a result of customer feedback, Pete has recognised the need for local rather than central decision-making. Decisions such as how to manage queues at busy periods, whether to spend time accepting and counting lots of small change and providing compensation for expenses arising from errors are all now empowered to local level, where the staff can make decisions for their area.

Another innovation, instigated by Pete is a "priority hotline" where senior staff members are the final decision makers on various areas of the operation. Every member of the staff has access to the hotline number to each of the senior decision makers and the call has utmost priority. This has resulted in calls being taken in board meetings. In Pete's view it is better to keep the directors waiting than a customer".

In Pete's view the real battle to provide really great customer service lies in how well the internal customer is dealt with. Most customer facing members of staff understand the need to provide great service and do their utmost to achieve this. When you move back to the people who serve the people who serve the customers, sometimes something gets lost. Perhaps some of the sense of urgency goes or maybe processes, procedures and rigidity in following the manual gets in the way of understanding customer needs.

This is the area where Pete is working on. He has introduced the concept of "Do not accept second best" and encourages staff to challenge colleagues if they feel that customer needs are being subrogated. Where members of staff feel that they have not received the best possible service from a colleague, they can quietly let Pete know their concerns and he will, with great diplomacy, see what he can do to improve matters.

Keeping up to date with customers through the panel members keeps Pete busy but he is always looking for improvements. He is always on the look out to keep customer focus at the top of the agenda by keeping things lively and interesting. Having discovered the correlation between branches with high staff satisfaction scores and those with highest customer satisfaction (yes, they are very much the same…. amazing is it not?) he has done much work to discover why some people and teams are better at service delivery than others and transferring the behaviours.

Exceptional service to Pete is always linked to:

1. Keeping promises

2. Limiting hassle

3. Keeping customers informed – right information at the right time and relevant to each customer (i.e. no blanket mail shots on new products)

4. Making customers feel like important and valued individuals.

At the beginning of this chapter it was stated that Pete saw the search for customer excellence as a pursuit not a destination. He remains in pursuit but in the meantime his efforts have helped make the Yorkshire one of the most admired customer service organisations in the world of financial services.

If asked to distil his success to just one element it would be, "asking customers what drives them to do business with you."

Herts Action for Disability – Welwyn Garden City

Having been discharged from hospital and unable to initially walk long distances, through partial disability, my friend was confined to a wheelchair. As a family man, his young children had to come to terms with Daddy leaving them in an ambulance one day and returning in a wheelchair a few months later (with regular hospital visits in between).

Things began to get back to normal, slowly, until one of his children began to develop uncharacteristic tantrums and unprompted mood swings. Probing one day, his wife revealed that their little girl was 'scared of Daddy's new wheelchair because it made him unable to play with her any longer'. His wife relayed this to their hospital Occupational Therapist, who suggested a visit to HAD at their base in Welwyn Garden City.

The visit was arranged one Saturday morning and the family duly arrived. Even though it was their first visit, HAD's CEO, Annabelle Waterfield, greeted them like old friends and eagerly listened to the story about their little girl. "I have just the thing" Annabelle quickly exclaimed, leaving them to explore for themselves.

She returned a little while later, obviously hiding something behind her back. Pointing to the little girl Annabelle went into the 'close your eyes, put your hands out' routine. With her eyes tightly shut the little girl duly put both hands out, ready to receive her anticipated surprise. On opening them she was presented with the sight of a Barbie doll sitting in her very own pink, plastic wheelchair, with all the details, just like Daddy's'.

The family returned home with their new Barbie in her wheelchair, generously given to them to borrow by HAD 'for as long as it takes'. Needless to say, Barbie and wheelchair became the little girl's favourite toy and her fathers own chair became less of a threat as more games were played.

The tantrums and mood swings gradually stopped. My friend was able to concentrate on getting better and family life began to return to normal.

Not only did HAD know exactly what to do that immediately communicated acceptance to the little girl but the way they did it retained my friend's dignity and demonstrated a genuine care for their customers.

Together with my friend, I have been along to see HAD at close quarters and they have many innovations there that specialise in assisting disabled individuals to gain back their self respect and live as near a normal life as their disabilities will allow.

They also are a non-profit making organisation that is offering what we consider to be true customer service for no financial gain, but in a truly professional manner."

Thank you to John Adams for this nomination.

WOW!
that's what i call service!

Retention of Customers

A 5% improvement in customer retention could lead to an increase of between 25% and 125% in bottom line profits!

Most businesses seem more concerned with attracting new customers rather than keeping existing customers. But here are some examples of businesses that are going to great lengths to keep their customers from leaving.

Reach out and touch – Garlands Call Centres

In April 2005, Chey Garland, founder and chief executive of Garlands Call Centres, was declared winner of the prestigious Veuve Clicquot Business Woman of the Year Award. The following day the national newspapers were full of stories of how she had risen from her beginnings as a market trader's daughter, leaving school at 16 without qualifications to develop a multi million pound business and becoming one of the north-east's biggest employers.

The story is, at first glance, a classic rags-to-riches tale, nourished by ambition, hard work and a determination to succeed. Few of the newspaper stories however captured the essence of Garlands' success

183

based upon outstanding customer service, starting with the staff and permeating through to the companies who outsource their work to Garlands and the end-user customers.

With nearly 3,000 staff based in five buildings in three centres and major contracts with clients such as Virgin Mobile, Vodafone and Wanadoo, Chey has built the business inside seven years and during this time it has established a reputation as one of the most dynamic and fast expanding companies in the country. The company has won many awards, including that of Customer Service Contact Centre of the Year and Customer Service Newcomer of the Year in the National Customer Service Awards, together with several appearances in various finals.

Right from the outset, Chey recognised that great customer service starts with the way that a company treats its internal customers – the staff and the company has also developed a reputation for the way it holistically supports and develops its people.   In addition to a full range of training programmes, an excellent performance appraisal system and great reward and recognition, all of which you might expect, they have instigated counselling and community based initiatives aimed at reducing absenteeism and attrition and developing life skills for tomorrow's team leaders and managers.

The catalyst for the "Touch" programme, as it has subsequently become known, was Chey's desire to know what really lay behind her absentee figures. Like most contact centres, Garland's suffered from a loss of productivity as a result of occasional days absenteeism. The pattern was familiar, one or two days here and there, often for minor illnesses. Chey did not believe it was malingering or a case of skivers conning a free day off, while at the same time she was not convinced that all of the illnesses were entirely genuine either. She noticed that included amongst the list of those with more than one absentee record during the period, were several of her most reliable and committed employees, who she firmly believed enjoyed and valued their jobs and would be unlikely to jeopardise them for the sake of an occasional day or so extra holiday.

Eventually she decided to conduct a highly confidential survey, including interviewing all the absentees over the period of the review. Staff that had been specially trained in interviewing and counselling skills conducted the interviews. The assurance was given at the outset that all information would remain confidential and that whilst management would learn the overall results of the survey, they would not be supplied with any details that could identify the team member concerned, unless the person specifically gave permission. Winning the confidence of staff was vitally important and Chey has made sure that at no time has that confidence ever been misplaced.

In some respects the findings might appear to be as expected, many of the lost days were due to drink and, sometimes, drug abuse. However, it was not the staff member who had over indulged but, in many cases, it was a member of the household, often a partner or spouse who had the problem and the staff member was a victim. In other cases it was the demands of aging and sometimes demanding parents who were the reason for the absenteeism.

Staff robbed of their money so that they did not even have the fare to work, staff nursing black eyes and other, more serious, bruising and staff coping with the needs of one or more sick members of their family were typical of the kaleidoscope of calamities that affected many of the team members. Chey was astounded at the range and magnitude of the problems facing so many of her staff and far from being put out by their occasional non-attendances, she admired their tenacity to keep going and she knew that they were the kind of people that she wanted in her team.

Whilst there was no magic wand that the company could wave to solve all the problems, Chey decided that there was some practical help that they could provide to assist staff and maybe alleviate the problems. She invested heavily in training for members of staff who were prepared to be volunteer counsellors and made sure that they were available on all shifts to help any member with problems. The trained counsellors were able to demonstrate that they understood the problems and sometimes just providing a listening service was enough to help. In other cases the counsellors were frequently able to offer support, practical advice or a referral to an appropriate agency.

As a result of the initiative, absentee rates have dropped to a level well below the average for contact centres and members of staff really appreciate the concern expressed for their well being. This has always resulted in improved staff retention rates. Retention is extremely important for growing contact centres like Garlands as replacement recruitment, together with the accompanying need for training, is a considerable drain on resources. Furthermore, loss of competent people whose knowledge and experience could play a significant role in the company's expansion could be an inhibiting factor to the corporate ambitions.

An ancillary benefit arising from this initiative was the developmental effect upon those volunteers who trained as counsellors. They grew as people through a greater understanding of the problems facing many of their colleagues. This and their growing confidence and ability in dealing sensitively with people issues has increased their value to the company as future leaders and managers - an important asset in a growing organisation.

The second - and equally important - strand to the "Touch" programme relates to the local community help programme, whereby

Chey allows staff members to work, on paid company time, within the local community on worthwhile projects. The range of projects is wide ranging and Chey will consider any project, provided it is genuinely worthwhile and that she can see the commitment of the member concerned.

One outstanding example is that of a young man who had worked at Garlands since leaving school. He had been very good at his job, was lively, self-confident and ambitious. He was looking at a team leader role, with a view to management but Chey felt that his vision was narrow and his focus was entirely self-centred. Chey knew that this was because the young man's life experience was somewhat limited. He had after all known only school and contact centre work – hardly a wide perspective on life.

The young man volunteered to work in a school for children with learning difficulties and was assigned a young boy who needed much attention and patience. One half-day a week for several terms, our contact centre tiger went to the school and helped develop his charge's reading skills. This required considerable patience – not one of the young mentor's natural attributes. Just gaining the trust of the boy took time and initially our volunteer found this very difficult. Gradually however the boy's reading ability improved and our hero could see the difference that he had made.

Once again we see an example of what appears to be an altruistic act by the company returning real benefits to the company as well as to the community. As Chey says the young man from the contact centre learned a lot about himself during his part-time secondment and that learning will stand him in good stead as he moves into supervisory roles within the company. Here is a good example of how the company is able to develop a young man with considerable potential, providing him with a wider experience than can be obtained within the normal environment but without the necessity to leave the company to gain that wider experience.

Of course the company's staff is involved in a much wider range of activities than that detailed above but all contribute to the community and develop individual and team building skills that have real value to Garlands. Additionally the company name is enhanced, within the community from where much of future staff recruitment will come.

Garlands are widely acknowledged as one of the country's fastest growing companies and one of the most successful contact centre businesses in the U.K. In an era when many organisations are exporting contact centre work to far away overseas destinations, in order to reduce costs, Chey and her management team have grown their business by winning contracts from major household name customers by demonstrating great results, a cost-effective return and outstanding service.

Garlands' contracts include all aspects of contact centre work. They undertake service and sales work on both an incoming and outgoing basis. Quite often they have undertaken a modest project on behalf of a customer and performed so well that the customer has subsequently awarded them larger contracts. Additionally, quite often the customer has incorporated Garlands' standards and procedures into their internal contact centres.

Chey knows above all that the Garlands success record can only be sustained and progressed if they are able to recruit, train, develop and retain committed and fulfilled staff able to provide a great service to the customers of their customers. It is not just a case of paying good salaries and incentives because whilst these are important, alone they will not provide job satisfaction, pride in achievement and commitment to the team.

Without all of the above, the task of building upon the success of an already highly successful company will prove impossible. Not only does the company need to develop the skill base of their staff and provide for tomorrow's leaders, they need also to retain the services of those performing basic roles and who, perhaps, do not seek a bigger role.

The "Touch" programme, with its diverse range of activities, provides a basis to provide many aspects of staff fulfilment and development. There is no mandatory element and the programme is entirely flexible in order to enable the staff to benefit in ways entirely appropriate to their needs and desires. It is imaginative and brave and already has returned real dividends to the company as well as to many employees and the wider community.

Are there any lessons to be gleaned from the experience of the "Touch" programme at Garlands?

- The first point to take note of is that absentee figures bear close scrutiny. The assumptions that many senior managers make about casual days off are not always correct. Real reasons might be even less palatable in some respects but may reveal the staff members concerned in a different light. Like so many problems, understanding the reasons is often a huge step towards finding a solution.

- Above average absenteeism and attrition are both expensive for a company and hold back growth plans in successful expanding organisations. Therefore it is worth investing in research and solutions aimed at minimising both these areas. Incidentally companies with high absenteeism often experience high attrition also.

- Staff development need not be restricted to conventional training and team building exercises. Widening life experiences and developing people skills outside the narrow confines of day to day work needs can pay huge future rewards in terms of building better prepared staff to cope with tomorrow's demands.

- Well thought out investment in the community, involving staff commitment, can reap dividends both in staff morale and well being as well as raising the positive profile of the organisation.

- No matter how outstanding, creative, hardworking and committed the senior management team are, a business based on providing great service to thousands of customers can only thrive through the efforts of the 'shop floor' staff. The business depends upon them and nobody understands this better than Garlands' principal, Chey Garland – the UK's Businesswoman of the Year who despite building a company from scratch has always been aware of the need to provide outstanding service to the people who will provide great service to the customers.

- Continuity and consistency. In 2006 Garlands were again successful in the National Customer Service Awards when Jennifer Lawson won the Customer Service Newcomer of the Year award.

1st Class Mail – Wisewood Post Office, Sheffield

Mark De Salis made the nomination. Here's what made him say, "WOW!"

"My wife, Karen, and I run our business from home and every evening we take our parcels to our local post office.

Our customers seem to expect 28 days delivery. They're always surprised when they receive their product the next day. We feel this is important, as we want our customers to receive great service.

Recently, I took 9 parcels for posting and only realised when I got to the counter that I'd left my money on my desk in the office. You can imagine my embarrassment and thought I'd be letting down our customers.

Sonia, the postmistress, immediately said, 'Don't worry, we'll post these today and you bring in the money with tomorrow's lot.'

Fantastic! My relief was obvious. Not only did all the parcels go on time, Sonia even gave me a receipt, as if I'd already paid.

Everything was sorted out the next day but what a great attitude and great service. People make the difference and Sonia and all the staff at Wisewood Post Office in Sheffield are a great example. As competition in the postal sector increases in the future, do you think I'll be using another service - No!"

Here's what I especially liked about this story:

Firstly, The WOW! Moment for Mark came about because of his own passion and commitment to service his customers. Just read what he says again. "…we want our customers to receive great service."

Just think about this. Mark's customers expect delivery in 28 days but they're surprised when they get delivery the next day. Mark has set himself a service standard to under promise but massively over deliver. And having achieved that standard every day he just didn't want to fail. Even though his customers would never have noticed!

In fact, Mark could have waited another 27 days to post these parcels and the customer wouldn't have noticed!

Because it was important to Mark to get the parcels sent, he got them sent. And he did it with the help of his supplier, Wisewood Post Office. If it hadn't been important to Mark do you think that the parcels would have got sent that day? I doubt it.

The second reason I like this story so much is because Sonia, the postmistress at Wisewood, took a very personal risk. I bet that there is nothing in the rulebook at the Post Office that allows someone to process some parcels and issue a receipt without taking any money. And yet, that's just what happened here.

The WOW! Awards is not about doing things to the rulebook. It's about those wonderful moments when someone takes a risk and does something off his or her own bat, something unexpected.

WOW!

Well done Mark and well done Sonia at Wisewood Post Office. Keep on delighting your customers.

WOW! Award on Tour – Grand Plaza Hotel, Singapore

We're breaking our own rules to give a WOW! Award to a hotel in Singapore. Occasionally we get such a passionate plea from a customer on behalf of an overseas business that we just have to give in.

Ken Everett is one of our members from down under. And he's a great fan of The WOW! Awards. Here's the story in Ken's own words:

I presented a WOW! Award to Scott Butcher and the staff of the Grand Plaza Hotel in Singapore because some people just create a service difference. Scott is one of these people.

I've used the Grand Plaza dozens of times over 5 years. So much so, I used to keep a permanent box in the baggage room with papers, runners, clothes, etc.

During this time, Scott left to manage a sister hotel for a year or so. Standards dropped. Some of my colleagues, regular visitors to Singapore, moved to another hotel.

One day, I walked back into the lobby, 'fresh' from London, and I knew something was different. I couldn't quite pick what it was, until I later saw Scott striding across the lobby.

He makes a difference in all the staff just by being there.

I could give many examples of what this means to me. Here's a simple one. On one trip from London, I met a friend from Australia at the Grand Plaza. He brought me a bottle of Vegemite, that funny-looking black spread Australians love to put on their toast.

We used it at breakfast during our stay, and left the bottle for my next visit. Now, it's automatically replaced whenever it gets empty, or reaches its use-by date! This has happened for 4 years now.

Dozens of little things like this make a big difference!

Ken presented the WOW! Award to Scott at the annual Christmas party, arriving as a surprise guest and making the presentation after a series of company awards were made. "I told them, this was the first presentation of a WOW! Award outside the UK," says Ken. "The staff was very pleased to get 'international' recognition. Scott was blown away! Today, the WOW! Award hangs proudly in the executive lounge. I know - I was back again last week."

Made to Order – Mair's Delicatessen, York

Mair's Delicatessen in York added a customer's choice to the menu and helped create a new recipe when the customer's dietary needs changed.

An illness prompted Helen Walbey to nominate her regular sandwich shop for a WOW! Award. Here's her story:

> "I work in York and ages ago a colleague recommended a local sandwich shop for lunchtime escapades.
>
> It is excellent; the choice is huge, all freshly prepared with top quality ingredients. The staff are very friendly and even when they are busy they find time to have a chat.
>
> They have two tables and a short 'eat in menu' as well as part of the shop being a deli and fresh fruit and vegetable shop. I have become a firm regular visiting two or three times a week but even with this excellent service I was still not prompted to write in.
>
> This all changed when I became ill. I was off work for some time and in the process had to stop eating meat. Last week I returned to work part-time and of course picked up my best

friend at work and headed to the sandwich shop. Not only did they remember me but were most concerned as to where I had been for the last three months. They also remembered the complicated off-the-menu sandwich I had every time. And they informed me they have now included it on their new menu selection that is currently being printed!

They were very disappointed I could no longer eat it and suggested alternatives, one of which I selected and it was perfect as always. There were at least ten people in the shop but they still made a bit of time to catch up with an old customer.

I went back today and was able to try a mouthful of an alternative filling that is totally yummy (spicy black eye bean and stilton pate) which I will now be having for lunch tomorrow.

The food and service has been, without question, excellent every single time I have eaten there. And so I really feel I ought to pull my finger out and nominate them for an award especially as my favourite sandwich will now be in print - even if I can't eat it!"

I wrote to Eric Mair of Mair's Delicatessens in Heworth Village, York to let him know that he'd been nominated for The WOW! Award and Eric called me up to say how delighted he was and that he looked forward to receiving his certificate.

I could sense from the tone of Eric's voice that this is a sandwich shop with a difference. Why not give them a visit next time you're in York?

A Case Study – Hiscox Cases, Staffordshire

Hiscox Cases won a WOW! Award for backing its products up with great service. It's a rare example of a manufacturing company (rather than a service company) scooping a WOW! Award.

When we talk about customer service, it's only natural that we think of service businesses rather than manufacturers. But Hiscox Cases shows that great service can start at the factory, inspiring customer loyalty and encouraging repeat business.

Here's what a customer had to say about Hiscox Cases:

> "15 years ago I bought a hand made guitar that came in a Hiscox case. These cases are made to a patented design and though there are two or three other makers of cases of similar quality in the world, they all cost about twice as much, as well as being nowhere near as good!
>
> In December 2002 the handle fell off my 15-year-old case, so I emailed Hiscox and asked if I could purchase a new handle. Almost by return I got a reply to say a kit for a new handle was in the post. It duly arrived a couple of days later, free of charge. It just made me say 'Wow'.
>
> This was not the first time I had been delighted by Hiscox, I had spoken to them before for help and found them very good. Remember they do not usually deal with consumers directly, but through stockists.
>
> More recently I emailed them to ask if they were going to start making cases for Baritone saxophones (I play both saxophones and guitars). Again I quickly got a very polite note saying they

have been thinking about doing this for a long time, but they are constrained by factory space, though they hope to be able to do it if they move to larger premises this year.

Not only are they a great British business with an innovative product that is incredible value for money, but their service also backs it up."

Stars of the Internet – Star

Companies are normally nominated for a WOW! Award after delighting one customer, but Star landed six nominations in very quick succession.

How did they do it? It turns out that Star have been telling their customers about The WOW! Awards and some of those customers have nominated the company.

Telling your customers about these awards is a powerful way to demonstrate your commitment to customer service. Star's customers had great things to say about its service, especially its technical support.

Ian Burton said:

> "They are all fantastic especially the help desk. You have a problem. You send in an email request. They call you back and fix it."

Mike Robinson from Komatsu UK told us:

> "Every time we deal with Star, the team as a whole is 100% professional in their approach and manner, totally efficient, extremely polite and helpful and 100% reliable. The best

decision we made when selecting the ISP for our company to use. We haven't had cause for one complaint and hope this continues."

Matt Valentine from Edale said:

"This company offers quite amazing tech support. They always get back to you within the hour and the staff are very polite, friendly and above all helpful. I've used many ISP and web hosts, but so far none have come even close to the quality of support from Star"

Richard Bevan at Royal Academy of Dance said:

"We were having firewall configuration problems and a Star support desk representative spent over 2 hours on the phone checking and reconfiguring the firewall. As this is an unmanaged service they went far and beyond the normal call of duty to ensure we could pursue other business opportunities. Star's help is always very prompt and their representatives very friendly / welcoming."

Gareth Stevens from Adsm put it like this:

"In the last three months we changed our ISP over and moved offices at the same time. The office move meant reconfiguration of our business network and how we connect to the internet, along with that it coincided with a change of ISP due to poor customer service and reliability (of the old ISP). We found that it was a huge task to undertake both of these changes at the same time but Star were there to help us. They were available on the phone constantly. If you left a message for them they would get back to you within 10 minutes, if you emailed them they would reply within minutes and they even helped us with non-ISP issues. I feel that the customer service offered by Star is so refreshing in this day and age and in this industry. I am so confident in their worthiness for this award that I am always recommending them to my customers and suppliers."

A Fishy Tale – The Lodge Hotel, Huddersfield

The Lodge Hotel in Huddersfield has won The WOW! Awards with a little help from the haddock.

They showed flexibility and delighted a customer who had this to say:

> "The food and service at the Hotel is outstanding. Friendly people, great cuisine and a good wine list to boot.
>
> One of our favourite dishes was smoked haddock with poached eggs for breakfast. The fish was succulent and the hollandaise sauce exquisite. We raved about this dish to a visitor who dropped by to see us at the hotel at 6.00 p.m.
>
> Having whetted her appetite, our guest asked if it would be possible to order the dish as a supper.
>
> I asked the receptionist who was extremely busy serving up a buffet for a large company meeting. But rather than give me the, 'Can't you see I'm busy?' look that is all too common in most hotels, he welcomed my request and set about organising the kitchen to create a breakfast dish in the evening.
>
> About 15 minutes later, the smoked haddock arrived, cooked to perfection with toast and a glass of wine. Our guest had

never tasted anything like it...and we had never come across WOW! customer service like it either!

We'll be back, needless to say."

Isn't it interesting how doing something a little out of the ordinary can generate such loyalty. Although this particular item was not on the menu at that time, it was presumably no more difficult to cook this dish that it would have been to prepare any other item that was on the menu.

Isn't it is also interesting how much enthusiasm customers have for saying thank you. This customer could have simply said thank you at the time. Or they could have left a small tip. But they actually decided to sit down and spend time writing a nomination.

I sometimes think that business owners underestimate the enthusiasm of their own customers.

Truth Breeds Loyalty – Firefly UK

Things don't always go according to plan, but one customer appreciated Firefly UK's honesty in telling him what's going on

Jon Morter nominated Firefly UK for The WOW! Awards. Here's what Jon had to say about this Internet Service Provider (ISP):

"I'd like to nominate my ISP, www.fireflyuk.net. They are a small ISP so occasionally they have problems the larger ones don't, yet they are so honest about it I have been impressed.

They have a had a big problem recently: It's all a bit technical but the company that supplies some of their dial-up numbers let them down so service was going to be poor over a weekend.

I've been prompted to nominate them because the email explaining what's gone on is incredibly honest and tells the customers exactly what's going on. If I have ever needed support from them I have got it, normally from a lovely guy called Ross. They are quick and very friendly too! I think this makes great customer service - honesty!"

This is the email that Jon received:

It appears that 08089909019/08089909889 has been turned off on us without our authority by our supplier.

This seems to be a direct result of us suggesting that we were considering moving our port supply away from them in favour of another supplier. Said supplier appears to have waited until our cheque to them had cleared before switching off our access number. This supplier had not contacted us to inform us and is not answering emails/phone calls/faxes.

We have already contacted our main supplier, replacement AND additional ports will be active on Monday reducing our already low contention ratio even further, we are actively pursuing these to be installed ASAP.

In the short term, over this weekend you may experience a number of redials as all customers attempt to login to either 08089996787 or 08089933286. I would ask you to be patient and considerate to all over this coming weekend and if you are not using your connection, please disconnect. To ease this a little, a 5 minute idle timeout has already been put in place.

Please bear with us over this very short period of inconvenience forced upon us by an unprofessional organisation that is obviously having serious difficulties at present.

Please be aware that this is in no way financially linked, we had just paid last month's bill on time, as always. FireFly remains financially sound and we are looking forward to increasing our capacity next week.

Thankfully, the forced departure of 08089909019/08089909889 sees the last of our indirect port agreements, with all current and future dealings being direct with the telecoms.

I would like to sincerely apologise for any inconvenience this may cause any of our customers but we are doing everything in our power to ensure that this problem is contained to the weekend. We thought it better if we were open and honest with our customer and let them know the situation as soon as we knew.

Please do not log support issues concerning connectivity issues over the weekend, they will be connected to the above and be resolved on Monday at the latest.

If you wish further support on this matter, please see our discussion forums at http://forums.fireflyuk.net

Kind Regards

Derek Lewis

We think that Jon is absolutely right. Trust is the most important factor in selecting a supplier. And honesty leads to trust.

What also fascinates me is that this is the second nomination Jon has made for The WOW! Awards. Jon himself is a branch manager for Richer Sounds - one of the best customer focused organisations that I know of. Isn't it interesting that Jon is always on the lookout for good service and doesn't hesitate to tell me about it?

A Big Step Forward – Special Feetures

Jane Raymond tells us how difficult it is to buy shoes for long and narrow feet and how much Special Feetures of Thames Ditton in Surrey value their customers.

> "No-one can imagine how difficult it is to buy shoes for long and narrow feet, except the people who have them!
>
> There are only a handful of such shops in the UK, but none I have experienced have such a personal caring service as Special Feetures. They keep shoe preferences and fittings on computer so are able to meet customers' requirements quickly and easily.
>
> Recently I purchased a pair of shoes which unfortunately started to 'unstitch' on the second wearing. On contacting Special Feetures they offered me my choice of refund, repair, exchange etc. Nothing was too much trouble. They paid postage for me to return the shoes and personally inspected the stitching repair before returning them, all within one week, AND gave me a credit on my account to compensate for the inconvenience.
>
> I have fought long and hard in the past to get shoe shops to accept my rights and their responsibility where faulty shoes are concerned, and this experience was pure pleasure in

comparison. I give full marks to Special Feetures for valuing their customers so highly.

I recommend them to all my tall friends!"

You would think that honouring a customer's legal rights would be a basic formality in any business. But clearly that is not the case and here is another opportunity to delight your customers.

WOW!
that's what i call service!

Culture

Break a stick of Blackpool rock at any point and it still says 'Blackpool'. Only when you have seen rock being made do you fully understand how that happens.

Only when you have experienced a business with an incredible customer service culture will you appreciate how that feels.

Food for Thought – Abel & Cole

Nothing is as likely to glue an organisation together – customers, suppliers, staff and proprietors, than a well publicised corporate mission and values statement to which everyone involved with the business can subscribe.

Producing such a statement is comparatively simple but demonstrating day by day the commitment to those ideals, for some, may be a different matter but not for Abel & Cole, a fast growing home delivery organic food company formed in 1988.

The business started as a baker's round but grew quickly through the range of product offerings and by spread of the geographic reach.

Fruit and vegetables, then meat and fish and now wine and beer have all been added to the range whilst deliveries, initially restricted to south London, now cover virtually the whole of southern England, stretching from Cambridge in the East to Bath in the west. More recently facilities have been established to extend the services to the Midlands and the North.

Each of the last five years has seen the turnover increase by over 50% and such rapid growth inevitably saw some breakdowns in service levels but with their commitment to excellence and teamwork, they quickly put the necessary improvements in place to re-establish an efficient delivery service.

This is a business that relies heavily upon customers being delighted with the service and the quality of the products, such that they not only re-order on a regular basis but that they also recommend the company to their friends. The company fully understands that, as much as customers enjoy the products, they will only recommend if they are confident that the service delivery will not put them in a position where they have to apologise to their friends for recommending the service.

In fact, the majority of new business comes from customer referrals. This and the consistent reordering by customers is testimony to their excellent customer service that led to the Abel & Cole Customer Service Team winning the 2006 Customer Service Team of the Year – General Award.

The company identifies six key elements as responsible for their successful customer service operation, which echoes throughout the whole operation.

1. Ethics of the company

The company's ethics undoubtedly attract both customers and staff who are drawn to the idea of organic food. The ethics encompass the ideals that farmers are paid a fair price for their produce, that staff are looked after and that the company has a regard for the environment.

2. Ownership and teamwork

Members of staff work as a team, sharing ideas and helping solve problems. They each take responsibility or ownership for any difficult situations that they encounter and they can do whatever they need to sort out customer issues. They can step outside company guidelines without authorisation or concern about recrimination. This policy enables them to solve issues quickly, maximising the prospect of retaining the goodwill of the customer, and move on to the next task.

3. Proactive approach to problem solving

The team is encouraged to anticipate problems that might occur and to provide solutions before these become issues. Weekly team meetings have provided the following improvements, all instigated by the customer service team.

- fragile stickers on delicate items to avoid damage in transit

- emails to customers, advising them of new product lines

- introduction of reusable wire baskets to reduce packaging

- advice on product care and usage through the newsletter. An example was when, after research and experimenting at home, a member of the team refused to accept that organic carrots go soggy because of the absence of chemicals and discovered that leaving them in water for an hour restored their firmness

4. Honesty and open communications

Each team member has a one-to-one meeting with their manager every quarter and the ratio of one manager to a maximum of seven reports is adhered to so that there really is time for this dialogue to be carried out and followed through properly. In addition there is a weekly team meeting and throughout the company there is an acceptance that things can go wrong, mistakes will happen but the important thing is open discussion to find future solutions.

5. Enhancing the role of the customer service team throughout the organisation

Realising that customer service does not exist in isolation within the company, the customer service team work closely with members from other areas of the company on a variety of projects. Customer service team members will be found well represented in the 'Green Team' – the body set up to review all environmental issues affecting the company. They also help marketing with the customer newsletter and launching new product lines. The recent organic wine range provides a good example and one where there was certainly no shortage of volunteers.

6. Environment

The team works in an excellent environment, the offices are light, open plan and airy. There is a CD player for music when required and members of staff are encouraged to take regular breaks away from their desks.

Perhaps the lunch club, to which almost all of the staff belongs, best sums up the environment and culture that exists at Abel & Cole. Each day, a member of the staff takes a turn at cooking lunch for everyone with another taking a turn to wash up. The enjoyment of the company products and each other's company provides a great platform to engender team spirit, idea sharing and the best possible product knowledge.

For a company like Abel & Cole, the mission values statement is more than part of a business plan but a way of life. The customers want real organic produce well delivered and, almost by definition, support the company's stance on the environment and ethics generally. Although the staff members do not have to be consumers of organic food in their personal lives, they understand the company's ethical viewpoint and would feel let down if the company departed from this for a short- term gain. For example, a decision to pay less than a fair price to a farmer for his produce, in order to achieve a short term price advantage to attract new customers.

How many organisations really live their values and demonstrate commitment to them on a regular basis? Abel & Cole clearly illustrate that a company that "eats together, grows together".

Plumbing New Depths –
Hemel Plumbing & Building Supplies.

This story illustrates how easily small local businesses can excel at customer service.

This is what Caroline Walford told me:

> "On Saturday I rang Hemel Plumbing & Building Supplies Ltd, looking to source a Franke sink and tap for a client at

extremely short notice. John Lewis had said the sink would take 4 weeks to get in! It is an unusual design. They were very helpful and confirmed prices and that they stocked a number of Franke products, and could arrange special delivery if required. So I went over in the afternoon to see them to discuss the requirements.

Whilst standing in the queue waiting to be served I watched a member of staff very patiently explain to a householder how to solve an unusual plumbing problem. He not only put all the bits together but also explained exactly what to do. Upon my turn I was greeted by name without opening my mouth (he had worked out who I was from the brochure I was holding). They were extremely helpful, wanted to know about my business as well as telling me about theirs when asked. They can source anything (including white goods). They confirmed they hoped to have the sink for collection on Tuesday, provided the manufacturer had it in stock. They would ring me Monday once they knew what the situation was.

They did phone me on Monday to confirm the sink had arrived. I collected it that afternoon - 24 hours ahead of the proposed schedule. Upon enquiring how they had exceeded my expectations, they confirmed they had faxed the order through to Franke on Saturday afternoon. (I had already tried phoning the manufacturer myself in the morning and they were closed).

The order was picked very early Monday morning and put on a special Securicor delivery. (They do a lot of business with Securicor.) This tells me they must have excellent relations with both Franke and Securicor to have achieved this. I rarely, if ever, have my expectations exceeded in this manner. I would not hesitate to recommend them to anyone. Their prices were also slightly cheaper than John Lewis, who I have found are pretty competitive. I am now opening an account with them."

When I went to present the award, I was gob-smacked by the level of care that was being given to customers.

The store was brilliantly laid out with fantastic displays of every possible piece of plumbing equipment. It's only a small store but one of the best presented that I've ever been into. Both Eddie Smith and Simon Carruthers clearly had a fantastic knowledge of their products and are so enthusiastic about what they do to help their customers.

Eddie did not know who I was or why I was there. He was busy trying to serve a customer with a replacement rubber washer for a ballcock when I arrived.

Eddie showed the customer a washer that he thought would be right but the customer said it was the wrong size.

The customer said that the washer he needed was the size of a 2 pence piece.

Eddie went into the back of the store and found a piece of rubber sheet. He then took a 2 pence coin form the till and used it as a template to cut a washer of the exact size.

Eddie gave the customer the washer and the 2p completely free of charge.

What I really liked was that Eddie was clearly having so much fun trying to serve this customer.

If ever I need anything to do with plumbing, there is only one place that I will go.

You Will Never beat us off the Pitch – Everton Football Club

Professional football, especially in the upper echelons of the Premiership, is not normally the place that you would look for great customer service. In fact we had a young lady in the Awards office who worshipped a famous London club that shall remain nameless.

'Why don't you nominate them for the National Customer Service Awards?' we asked one day after she eventually came off the phone after an interminable call trying to get tickets, for a big match for which her status as a regular fan entitled her to a lottery chance.

'Because they treat us fans like shite,' came the acerbic reply.

Well it is unlikely that you would get that response from an Everton supporter as the club really leads the way in customer service. Their customer service manager, Leigh McLean, won the Customer Service Complaints Manager of the Year Award in 2006 having been a finalist the previous year.

"For the moment, you might beat us on the pitch, but you'll never beat us off it," she says with pride as she and her team of four provide great service day in and day out.

Leigh is a true Scouser – from a family of Liverpool supporters, who knew relatively little about football before taking the job of building a customer service operation at Goodison in 2004. Since then she has fully embraced the culture at Everton, the club that really lives up to its self promoted reputation of being the family club.

It is interesting that the Premiership club (other than Everton) that Leigh herself rates as being good at customer service is Manchester City. Like Everton, who rank second in their city to Liverpool in terms of silverware, Manchester City has had to play second fiddle to Manchester United. You only have to remember the 'Avis, we try harder' scenario to see the parallel and customer service devotees will hope and expect that one day their foresight will help turn the tables in terms of playing success.

When it comes to complaint handling Leigh takes care of everything, apart from those relating to football matters like 'fire the manager' or 'buy some new strikers'. This is just as well because when she returned from honeymoon in 2004 she found 400 email complaints......all referring to the club's decision to sell Wayne Rooney.

However she cannot completely disassociate her role from the playing performance because her carefully constructed graphs demonstrate quite clearly the correlation between playing success and the number of customer complaints received. It appears the fans are much more forgiving of stanchions obstructing views and dodgy pies when the team is doing well than when they are on a poor run.

Whilst this makes planning an imprecise art, Leigh takes it all in her stride. She understands the passion of the fans, knowing that the club is not just part of their lives but often part of their family culture and heritage.

Leigh is also aware that on many occasions she has the power to make customers extremely happy. "Who's your son's favourite player?" she might coo to a fan after settling his query. She will then send the boy a signed item from the player in question, quite over and above the already accepted complaint resolution. On other occasions she might arrange an accompanied visit to the club's training ground to watch the players train and even meet them after the session.

During an average season, Leigh will arrange for 500 signed photos to be sent and will arrange 100 visits to the club's training ground at Bellefield.

To Leigh and the management team at Everton, customer service is much more than just providing popular sweeteners when things go wrong. They really value their supporters as customers to be satisfied on every occasion that they touch Everton, whether it is attending a game, making a purchase from the club shop or visiting the club's website.

They anticipate the needs of customers and endeavour to delight them with the service every time. They do not ride roughshod over the regular fans, who are fanatical about the club and who can be relied upon to support the club through thick and thin, but demonstrate their appreciation of that support and refuse to take it for granted.

A good example is that Everton, like most top clubs, sometimes find that matches against lesser lights in the league do not always sell out and consequently they make special offers to attract new fans. Everton realise that this is not completely fair on season ticket holders who commit themselves to every match for a substantial amount at the beginning of the season without knowing how well the team might play.

To compensate for this they have designed an attractive range of added value benefits, such as invitations to lunch at the club to meet the management and some of the players.

Everton are really committed to their fans and to their community. They take seriously diversity issues, facilities for disabled fans, development, education and encouragement of young players and their football in the community programme.

For Everton, football is not just a business based around a particular sport but it is part of the community. Everywhere that they touch with their customers, they try to be the best in each activity from match day programmes to quality of their website. In most of these there are league tables and awards and it is usual to see Everton at, or very close, to the number one spot every time.

On-the-field success in football may be transient – indeed, Everton have experienced a feast and famine spell in recent seasons – but the club is consistent in its approach to its customers and this will help build a loyal fan base that will stick by the club through thick and thin. Eventually this will translate to even better team performances and long term success.

Success on and off the field is definitely what Everton deserve – "Come on you blues" - and that from a Leyton Orient supporter. (Editor's note: Don Hales, author of this paragraph, supports Leyton Orient).
Professional and Fun – Mark Holt & Co, Plymouth

Delighting customers, creating a happy team and having lots of fun!

Mark Holt & Co of Plymouth has demonstrated that it is possible for a professional firm to also provide outrageously good customer service.

They are the latest winners of The WOW! Awards and are clearly committed both to their internal customers as well as their external customers.

Steve Vosper of S. R. Vosper told us, 'After Mark Holt & Co ran training for my firm, turnover has more than doubled, employees have gone from 2 to 7, and I'm now enjoying a better quality of life.'

And Steve was not the only delighted customer. Here's what David Whitehead of Stage Electrics had to say.

"In the four years of working with you, we have gained tax savings, created business ideas, and devised and implemented a strategy for the future adding in excess of £1m to the value of the company."

What particularly impressed judges at The WOW! Awards was the feedback from employees of Mark Holt & Co.

Kay Mortimore has been with the firm for 4 years. "I would never have believed (probably like most people) that it was possible to work for a firm of Accountants and have fun - but I was wrong! I can honestly say that over the past 4 years, Mark Holt & Co. have helped me to grow both professionally and personally and I hope will continue to do so for the next 4 years. I feel proud that I can say I am part of the Mark Holt team and the opportunities that I have been given have more than exceeded my expectations."

And the firm is clearly committed to having fun. Events for their customers have included Friday 13th Olympics, Easter Bunny Hunt, eating jelly and ice-cream with their hands, plasticine modelling and table tennis on the board room table.

Wouldn't you like to go and work for a company that has this much fun?

All Aboard the Heathrow Express

The customers at Heathrow Express are far more time conscious than almost any other railway passengers as the train company's service is a premium brand service from London to Heathrow operating a service every 15 minutes that reaches Heathrow in just 15 minutes.

The team at Heathrow Express goes to great lengths to get their customers to their destination as safely and quickly as possible.

Customer service plays a big part in the service delivery. Getting things right first time and swiftly dealing with situations that could lead to delay are important factors in running the service to time but just as important is the ability to react well when things do go wrong –something that is inevitable in the railway business, often for reasons outside the control of the railway operator.

In 2006, as well as winning the Customer Service Team of the Year Award for Transport & Distribution, Heathrow Express went on to be declared the overall winners of the main award of The Customer Service Team of the Year. There were a number of outstanding strategies and activities that led to this accolade but two, their behavioural pattern recognition training that gives staff the tools to quickly identify a customer who needs help, and their policy of train driver recruitment illustrate the lengths that they go to in order to provide the very highest levels of service possible.

The behavioural pattern recognition was introduced before 7/7 to not only help spot possible terrorist activity but also, by passive observation and casual interaction, to assist customers who might be unsure of their correct destination for their terminal or need other assistance, without the need to ask.

As far as train driver recruitment is concerned, the company has a policy that could be transferred to many other businesses in many sectors to enhance the understanding of customer needs. For many organisations, customer service fails not with the attitude or behaviour of frontline staff but with a lack of real understanding and response from those who provide services, often of a technical nature, without very much direct contact with the public.

Historically there has never been a shortage of young people wanting to be train drivers but not very many cite being a customer service professional as an ambition at an early age. Well at Heathrow Express, you cannot be one without the other!

No one at Heathrow Express joins the company as a train driver. If you aspire to such a role, you must start by being recruited as a customer service representative and your duties will be working face to face with customers on the platforms and on board the trains. Duties include directing passengers to the right section of the train according to their terminal, helping with queries and luggage and checking tickets.

After six months the new recruit can then apply to go on the course for train driving and, if he or she possesses the right aptitudes the training commences. Even having qualified as a train driver however, the staff member will continue to spend time working as a customer service representative as well as driving trains. A typical day might start with an hour or so working on the platform at Paddington, then driving a train to the airport, followed by a stint working in a ticket office before finishing the day by driving a train back to Paddington.

Apart from giving the company great flexibility when planning staff requirements at various times, the system results means that Heathrow Express is a united team who really understand customers. In the event of unforeseen delays and cancellations the company can utilise the maximum number of ready trained staff to keep the customers informed and as soon as the trains are running again, they can utilise extra driver capacity.

This is a team whose members came in voluntarily during 7/7 to see how they could help. The customer focus is absolute and there are so many other organisations that could benefit from multi-skilling technical or backroom staff so that they can help customers in special situations and have a deep understanding of their needs when performing their normal role.

Only the Best – Prêt a Manger, Bluewater

Prêt a Manger has been one of my favourite stores for a long time. As well as their food being fantastic it is always such a joy to shop there. Their enthusiasm, and the way that they communicate with their customers, is truly outstanding.

So I was delighted when we received a nomination for their store at Bluewater. But nothing could have prepared me for what I was about to read.

As you may know, Prêt is what I would call a 'self select store'. As you go into the shop, all of their beautiful fresh sandwiches are arranged in chiller cabinets along one wall together with their fresh fruit juices and fruit deserts.

The idea is that you walk along one side of the store selecting the products that you would like to buy. And when you reach the far end of the shop, there is a counter from which you can purchase a range of teas and coffees and pay for your purchases.

On this occasion, a customer first selected several sandwiches and took them to the till to pay. Our nominator happened to be stood in the queue behind her and watched what happened.

> "As I took my place in the queue I became the third person waiting to be served. The till operator saw that now he had more than two customers to help and immediately called for another till operator to help serve them.'

As I stood waiting for my turn I was fascinated to watch what was happening. This particular customer had picked out four different sandwiches from the chiller cabinets. The till operator carefully put all four sandwiches by the side of his till. He described each sandwich as he entered the price into the till and then placed each sandwich carefully into a carrier bag.

The first two sandwiches were processed and put into the bag without any problem. But when it came to the fresh salmon sandwich, he held that one back and said to the customer, "I'll change that one for you".

The customer was clearly a little surprised and intrigued about why this sandwich needed to be changed. After all, she had selected this herself. The till operator then went on to say, "This sandwich is not quite full with salmon and we like to see all our fresh salmon sandwiches simply bursting with fresh salmon".

The customer was absolutely staggered. And so was I.

I had never before seen a shop assistant take such care over items that the customer themselves had chosen to buy. In a fast food outlet, such service is completely above and beyond the normal call of duty. This is why it qualified for the WOW! Factor."

I was absolutely enthralled by this particular nomination it beautifully captures several elements that are absolutely fundamental to outstanding customer service.

First of all, there is the ongoing communication between the till operator and his customers. He immediately called for somebody else to help serve when he realised that he had more than two customers at his till.

He then read out the name of each of the sandwiches as he entered the price into his till. It's just such a nice way of confirming for the customer what it is that they are buying and maintaining communication. It also gives him the opportunity to enhance the buying pleasure. Hearing the words "fresh salmon sandwich" makes you feel good about this sandwich before you have even had the chance to taste it.

And then there was the offer to change one of the sandwiches. He could so easily have let the customer purchase this particular sandwich. And the customer would probably never have been any the wiser. But by drawing attention to it in this way he emphasised how much care and attention is taken at Prêt A Manger to get things exactly right.

In effect what this young man had done was to implement Prêt A Manger's guarantee before the customer had even realised that there was a problem. Guarantees are such a powerful way of reassuring our customers.

And finally, research has indicated that more than 70% of customers feel more loyal towards a business that has remedied a problem to their complete satisfaction than they were before the problem arose. Imagine how good this customer felt about having a problem resolved before she even knew about it.

Novotel London West – Service Extraordinaire

Built in the early 1960's, for many years the Novotel London West held an unrivalled position as London's premier exhibition and conference hotel. Today it offers state-of-the art conference, exhibition and event facilities with 5500 square metres of highly adaptable space, 31 meeting rooms, 629 bedrooms, 2 restaurants, 2 bars and 24 hour room service. A business and leisure hotel, at any one time they can be looking after over 4,000 guests.

In truth, in the early days, there was very little opposition as virtually the only comparable exhibition and conference facilities, on the scale that could be offered by the hotel, were to be found at the traditional purpose built exhibition venues and these were largely rather old and tired.

As a result business flourished as major events flocked to the newer hotel that could offer modern facilities and, of course, accommodation on the premises. Although the venue kept busy, it was not in those days a hotel noted for the customer experience. In truth the business kept flowing in and the staff did what was necessary to process the events and the guests.

Gradually there was a change in the market. London saw the opening of many more large conference venues, with modern facilities, including those that offered hotel accommodation. Suddenly the competition became much more intense and Novotel had to change in order to win and retain their business.

About this time, Rene Angoujard, was appointed as General Manager. Rene brought with him the experience of some twenty-five years experience within the group and more importantly the trust and respect of the Accor Hotels Group (Novotel is part of the Accor Group – a worldwide organisation owning over 10,000 hotels.) Rene was renowned for his passion and vision and his remit was simple – to turn the situation around and make Novotel London West Hotel and Conference Centre a flagship property in the group's portfolio.

Rene has always had a simple philosophy for running hotels based on great customer service. His belief is that providing respect and happiness for customers will always result in profits for the hotel. In Rene's words,

> "Good service is the cornerstone of success; good service brings more sales; good service brings more profit"

Two other favourite quotations of Rene's are:

> "The customer is not always right but treat them as though they are and this will keep them happy and you sane,"

> and

> "Find a job that you love and you'll never work a day in your life again."

Because of the regard in which he was held within the group, Rene had the freedom to introduce changes and invest in training with full support and without outside interference but his reputation was on the line.

He knew that the culture had to change to one based on delivering great customer service, first time, every time to every guest. He also knew that he could achieve very little on his own and appointed three fantastic ambassadors to spearhead "Service Extraordinaire". He chose his one personal assistant, the HR manager and the Training Manager – three young women who shared his vision and values.

Their vision was to create a service culture that would result in the Novotel London West being regarded as the best hotel in London and the best Novotel worldwide. This was a particularly bold vision statement at the time, given their starting position where very few guests would be likely to comment on a memorable visit.

They began by evaluating the current position and setting the learning objectives. They then set about creating awareness and gaining commitment from the employees.

The first phase was the introduction of hotel standards:

1. Look professional, be professional

2. Greet every guest and colleague

3. Look after your hotel

4. Be positive"

No rocket science there but straightforward guidelines that could be understood, accepted and followed by everyone. As always, it was the follow-through and implementation that was important.

At this stage the leaders undertook training with Mary Gober International so that they could develop their in-house training using the "Gober Method".

During the stage, the team developed some basic standards of appearance and manners that would become the hotel's standards. They involved the employees in discussions about appearance standards including hair, jewellery, uniform, grooming and make-up to arrive at an acceptable level designed to impress customers and present a professional image.

The next phase was to roll out training across all departments. They devised a highly interactive and fun three-hour training session under the "Service Extraordinaire" banner to all staff members. They did morning sessions, afternoon sessions, night shift sessions and Sunday sessions to ensure that every person at the hotel, from front of house to back-office and including all key suppliers and all agency staff went through the change of culture learning and could identify with the new standards and participate in the new cultural revolution. "Service Extraordinaire" became a powerful brand within the hotel

During the training they introduced the ten service behaviours that were to be developed in the weeks and months ahead:

1. Give customer assurance – first time, every time

2. Be well mannered and always gracious

3. Always repeat key information

4. Be open-minded, jump the obstacles

5. Cushion the blow

6. Give time, all the time, on time, every time, at the right time

7. Don't hold it, pass it to the right player

8. Be thankful

9. Keep the guest informed

10. Apply the finishing touch

The final part of the initial launch was the appointment of ten coaches, drawn from the various departments. The coaches were not chosen for their position within their departments but for their attitude and enthusiasm. The coaches do not train as such but act as ambassadors, supporting the staff throughout the hotel and reinforcing the standards and behaviours. In practice however, every staff member is a coach as all are encouraged to challenge any colleague, irrespective of status, to offer friendly advice on any aspect of the service behaviours, including dress, appearance and attitude.

One of the most imaginative training sessions related to the "5 Kitchen Senses". This comprises a series of unique and interactive demonstrations – using food as the medium, harnessing advanced technology to an exploration of the effects our senses have on our perception and enjoyment. Through this educational module comes a wider appreciation of the impact a customer's five senses have on their experience of the hotel and why the tastes, sounds, smells and sights that they encounter at the venue will help to create their perception of the hotel. With this understanding the staff can consider this as part of their role in delivering Service Extraordinaire and create a positive perception.

The project then entered the "Forming, Storming, Performing and Norming" stages, when the training was bedded down as regular behaviour. The three architects, despite all holding challenging 'day jobs' met at least once a day to discuss issues and progress and the coaches met weekly. New staff members joining after the launch were also given the initial training, just as soon after joining as possible.

Ongoing personal development of the team is provided for through the five key values of the hotel, which are part of Service Extraordinaire. The values are:

1. Transparency – we are open and honest with each other. All individuals are valued and respected.

2. Trust – we trust our employees to make informed decisions but recognise that sometimes they will make mistakes. All we ask is that they learn from them.

3. Professionalism – we encourage our employees to develop to their full potential. Receiving all the support needed to be a true "hospitality professional", ensuring the commitment to our guests.

4. Responsibility – we encourage our employees to take the initiative with our guests and to take ownership for guaranteeing their satisfaction at all times.

5. Innovation – we welcome ideas and creativity and will consult with employees in areas that involve them.

The long-term aim is to drive up standards in the UK's hotel and hospitality industry by raising the career potential that exists in hotel work. By making a career in the industry an attractive option (as it is in many parts of the world, including mainland Europe) it will attract more committed and talented people and standards will rise further. At the hotel staff are encouraged to develop their skills, including those not directly related to their immediate roles (such as learning a language or even learning advanced driving skills) and a great deal of learning material is made available and can be requested if the subject matter is not currently held.

Incidentally, members of staff are recruited primarily for attitude on the basis that most of the skills needed are capable of being taught but attitude is hard to change. Rene believes he can usually tell within the first 30 seconds whether a candidate has the right attitude. All new members of staff have the opportunity to experience life as a guest.

For a minority of employees, the new culture was difficult to accept. The new behaviour standards may have seemed somewhat dictatorial to some but, for the most part, the enthusiasm and excitement of the others pulled the doubters along until they saw the effects of the changes and themselves became converts.

It was the staff take-up that determined the success of the whole operation. The 250 plus staff come from over 50 countries and, as is common in the hotel industry, several are relatively short-term employees as they see hotel work as a good way to see the world. However "Service Extraordinaire" captured their imagination. The training was fun and the message was simple. As most members of hotel staff enjoy serving customers, once it was clear that everyone was involved and committed; they quickly started pulling out all the stops.

Naturally, they continued to invest in skills training for the various roles within the hotel, conference and exhibition environment but "Service Extraordinaire" remained the cornerstone of the hotel's culture. Recruitment was restricted to people with the right attitude, people who would fit in well with the new highly effective and motivated team.

One of Rene's demands for the new initiatives was that they had to be measurable. Of course, hotels have all sorts of measures relating to occupancy rates, conference booking records and standard guest feedback forms. Rene, however, wanted something faster that could give instant feedback and allow any perceived shortcomings to be acted upon immediately.

What they wanted was some simple measurable factors that could be easily understood and incorporated into their daily lives and this led to the development of "Qualisurvey" a customer satisfaction survey completed by the Service Extraordinaire leaders by face-to-face interviews with ten random customers and comprising ten standardised questions relating to their stay at the hotel. The survey is conducted either during the customer's stay or at time of departure. The results are analysed and distributed daily so that all departments and all their team members have instant feedback as to how the hotel and the various key areas are performing. Any shortcomings can be corrected within an hour.

Very quickly staff could see such comments as "it seems the main aim of all your staff is to bring a smile to the face of their guests". Such feedback inspired the team to maintain their new standards, as they were able to see the effect it was having on their customers.

The next measurement, "Qualivision" reflects the guests' satisfaction after their stay covering eight areas – basics, technicalities, lunch/dinner, breakfast, service, atmosphere, value for money and overall satisfaction. This is evaluated through telephone surveys or self-evaluation. Each question has a score from one to ten so that relative performance can be gauged on a regular basis.

Another measure "Resavision" provides a measured result of the quality of the reservation booking service. The reservations are evaluated through pseudo-reservations made by an outside company and are measured for welcome/friendliness, basics, reassurance, identification of a new customer and sales.

The results of both Qualivision and Resavision are published regularly on the intranet alongside previous results for comparison.

Other feedback analysis include "Signature" to monitor sales calls, guest comment cards left in bedrooms, restaurant questionnaires and the Meetings, Incentives, Conference and Events (MICE) Tracker to de-brief every event held at the venue.

The results were immediate and quite stunning. Before Service Extraordinaire, customer satisfaction was showing at just under 80% and within a year after its introduction was recording 98%. Complaints were down by an astonishing 92% and staff retention improved threefold - going from rather below average for London hotels to far better than average in what is renowned for being a high turnover job market.

In 2003 the Service Extraordinaire team won the Training Team of Year Award in the National Customer Service Awards. Since then many accolades have followed including Customer Service Team of the Year - Leisure & Tourism in the 2006 Awards. Their commitment to excellence has taken many different directions and they became the first and, to date, only hotel to be certified ISO 14001 for environmental practices.

The hotel as a whole, with active participation from employees, supports local charities, schools, arts and council initiatives.

Service Extraordinaire has continued to deliver results right from inception and the quest continues. Most importantly, from the business perspective profitability is up 10% year on year, a remarkable achievement when set against the background of the problems that have beset that industry in recent years and Service Extraordinaire is now being rolled out across the rest of the Novotel chain in Europe.

There are many lessons that can be gleaned from this chapter and you do not have to be in the hotel business to benefit from them.

- When attempting to change culture, it is important to do it thoroughly. Half-hearted approaches will not do. Some tough decisions will need to be made but staff will buy-in when they see the reasons, understand the benefits and start to enjoy the feeling of striving to be the best.

- Measurement of improvement is important. Novotel did not go for reams of complex figures that take ages to produce and are capable of multiple interpretations. They went for a fast daily measure that could give an instant reading and an opportunity to act on any under-performing areas before they became a major problem.

- At Novotel London West, everyone was involved in the training sessions from the General Manager down. It is vital to have the total commitment of top-level management, if a real service culture is to be sustained. This does not just mean directors approving the plans and providing the budget but really taking part and demonstrating by their personal actions that they are a part of the cultural change.

- Following from the above, Novotel included all agency staff in the training and staff of any suppliers working on the hotel's premises. They recognised that the customers do not care who works for whom – they just want great service.

- A cultural change programme of this nature demands time, money and resources to be successful. Novotel invested wisely – the three initiators underwent outside training and trained as trainers to pass the message on – and made sure they put in the time and energy to follow through continually.

WOW!
that's what i call service!

Revenue

Some businesses are concentrating so hard on the score board that they forget about playing the game.

But when you focus on what motivates your customers, that is when you will achieve the sales and profits that you really want.

These are some examples of business that have generated incredible loyalty, repeat business, sales and profits.

Cardiff gets the WOW! Factor – Slater Menswear, Cardiff

I visited the Slater Menswear in Cardiff to present them with their certificate.

This was the first business in Wales to win The WOW! Award.

I just couldn't believe it what was happening.

The customer who nominated Slater had already told me about the outstanding range (including half sizes), superb value, free alterations (even if you put on weight after buying a suit) and sweets on the counter.

And I found a whole lot of other things that really blew my mind.

Free coffee.

Leaflets in a variety of languages - including Icelandic!

A prize draw for customers.

And even a shot of best Scotch whisky!

I had to keep reminding myself that this was a clothing store. I was in danger of believing that I was on holiday!

Customer Service – the Star of the Show

Sometimes one comes across businesses where the delivery of the promise is so much in the hands of specialists that supporting staff may feel that their efforts are so secondary to the main undertaking that providing outstanding service would be superfluous. In fact this is rarely the case and the story of the former Clear Channel Entertainment theatre division - now known as Live Nation - provides a great example.

This is a chain of theatres and conference venues, some in London's West End and many in provincial towns throughout the UK.

Until a few years ago, they thought that the success of the operation largely depended upon the quality and reputation of the show – it might be a blockbuster like 'Phantom of the Opera' and on occasions perhaps a less well-known and less popular show.

They thought that their main function was negotiating with the production companies to get the best shows into the theatre on the most favourable terms and beyond that, all they had to do was manage the box office, show people to their seats and maintain the fabric of the building.

Then a couple of years or so ago, they decided to see what difference they could make by overlaying superb customer service on top of the show. Now obviously in this kind of business results will take a long-time to come through. But they reasoned that if they gave great customer service to ensure a fantastic night out, customers might come back to the theatre and recommend friends even when the following show was not such a popular attraction and maybe, if you make every thing welcoming and easy for them, they just might spend more when they are at the theatre.

At the forefront of the initiative was Denise Aldridge, a lively lady with an irrepressible personality. Although not directly involved in show business herself, her background included spells as a holiday camp redcoat and as an overseas-based holiday representative working with the 18 - 30 customer age group.

Many of the staff at theatres are attracted by the nature of the business and were ready and willing to take part in the new approach and Denise was just the right person to provide the training, the motivation and the impetus to get the new show 'on the road'. Her efforts won her the 'Customer Service Trainer of the Year' in 2005.

Denise and her colleagues looked at every facet of customer service from making it easier to obtain interval drinks, organising taxis at the end of the show and ensuring that staff became part of the night's entertainment – even dressing in context with the show itself.

They did this at every one of their sites and two years later all were able to report increased attendances and uplifts in spend per customer on the night. Naturally, over two whole years there would be a host of other factors that could affect results - including the economy, the weather and the perceived quality of the shows - but the fact that every theatre in the group showed substantial improvements against a background of flat attendances in the theatre world generally, indicates the level of impact that the customer service initiative had on this group.

The figures below, showing the improved results over a two-year period, relate to just one of the theatres - a small provincial site with committed and enthusiastic management.

Customer Satisfaction index	up 15%
Theatregoers	up 37%
Performances	up 25%
Attendance per show	up 11%
Spend per theatregoer (excluding admission)	up 12%
Total Revenue (including admission)	up 38%

Although this is just one of the theatres in the group, each and every one of them had a similar story to report. Some had above average increases in attendances whilst others showed greater rises in the spend per visit but all showed positive increases as a result of the approach to service.

So here we have clear and calculable evidence of great customer service making a positive contribution to the bottom line. In summary for the venue illustrated - a 15% increase in customer satisfaction has led to a 38% rise in revenue and, we can safely assume that much of the extra revenue will go straight to the bottom line as very little extra expenditure has been incurred.

Other benefits resulting from this initiative?

- Production companies are happy and more likely to offer their productions to venue

- Staff more involved

- Theatre group's reputation is growing

Great actors performing in a fantastic production can thrill an audience but customers may choose to remember the ambience, the greeting, the friendliness of the staff, the convenience of arrival and departure and ease of buying interval drinks as much as the performance. These factors are likely to be even more influential in the decision to return to the venue for the next show. After all the customer knows the show itself will be different but will expect the hygiene factors – good or bad – to be the same and this will, in many cases be the deciding factor.

There are many other situations where the prime delivery is essential – one can think of hospitals, dentists, repair businesses and sporting venues. In each and every case the performance of the support staff, can be as influential in the final assessment of satisfaction as the main delivery. This may or may not be rational but it is factual. After all, most customers are more able to judge the competency and helpfulness of a receptionist than the skills of the mechanic.

If you do not believe this, just look at the results of our theatre group. Did they write or produce the shows? Did they act and sing on stage?

Absolutely not, but they upped their customer service game and results improved everywhere.

Fresh Produce, Fresh Thinking – Brookfield Farm, Aston End, Stevenage

Brookfield Farm delights customers with daring recipes that tingle the taste buds and show them how to make the most of their purchases.

Brookfield Farm Butchery & Village Stores in Stevenage is the latest winner of the prestigious WOW! Award for customer service.

This is what one of their customers had to say about the shop:

> "I had been aware of the shop for a long time but never bought anything until one day I decided to take a look inside. I was certainly impressed by the display of meat and decided that we should try something.
>
> That first joint of beef was so tender that it just melted on the tongue. All my family enjoyed it and we decided to go back the following week.
>
> What we love about this shop is not just the quality; it's also the service that we get.
>
> The butchers are always happy to advise me on what cuts to buy and how to cook them. We've experimented with cuts of meat that we'd never even heard of before and every one has been delicious.
>
> We've been encouraged to be more adventurous with our recipes and buying from this shop is always so much fun. We always have a good laugh and a joke while still getting great

service. In fact, we enjoy going to this shop so much that my family comes with me whenever they get the chance."

We've told lots of our friends about Brookfield Farm and we know that they are now buying there too."

If every shop in the UK gave this level of service we would not only delight our UK customers but all our overseas visitors as well.

Tower 42 – Reaching to the sky

Imagine that you are going to stay at a luxurious five-star hotel – the best that money can buy.

You would anticipate being greeted personally, warmly and with polite efficiency. If there were security issues you would want them to be dealt with carefully, thoroughly and with courtesy.

Naturally you would expect the establishment to be spotlessly clean, impressively styled and everything, such as lifts and escalators, working perfectly. You would take for granted room service, alarm calls, deliveries of newspapers, provision of internet services if required and a good choice of fine dining options.

Finally you might well want to work out in a well run leisure facility, take a swim, maybe visit the hairdresser and perhaps have need to use the property's own discreet transport, possibly to take you to the theatre to see the hottest show in town with tickets procured by the helpful concierge.

Yes, you would probably expect all this and more from a five-star hotel but what about at your office?

Okay so you do not normally expect such service from your place of work. The necessary security is in place but the personnel change frequently and whilst polite enough, perform the function in a 'jobsworth' sort of way. The receptionist is chirpy, gum chewing and uninspiring and shows little interest in you or the work of your organisation. Often things break down and they take time to repair – that is just the way it is.

If you want a sandwich at lunchtime you go up the road for it and queue with everyone else and you might as well get your haircut while you are out because no-one is going to do it on the premises – come on, this is the office we are talking about!

Five-star hotels are one thing and office blocks another. Each fulfils a different function and ordinarily there is little point comparing the service of one with the other. They are planets apart. Try and ask the caretaker or receptionist to get you tickets for the latest show to hit your local theatre and you will be sectioned off and spend the next twelve months undergoing psychiatric treatment.

It is the way of the world!

Well not so at Tower 42, London's distinctive office landmark – formerly the NatWest Tower – where they have revolutionised office facility management by introducing five-star hotel service and standards to their tenants.

The story started in 1998 when the new company Tower 42 – a partnership between investment bankers and a property company – acquired the 42-storey building, at the time London's tallest office block. The premises were just 30% occupied and there was nothing special about the building, other than its sheer size, or the facilities offered.

Right from the start a new vision was born. Tower 42 was going to introduce new standards in office facilities management based on five-star hotel service standards. Rents would be high – just about the highest in the country – but the building was situated in the financial centre of London where high rents are endemic.

The building was completely refurbished and in the process many of the common facilities such as reception, lounge and conference areas were imaginatively re-landscaped to make them attractive features rather than dead, drab areas. They created exciting areas, oozing quality and visually dramatic.

They were equally innovative in the introduction of flexible leasing strategies, again breaking the mould of industry norms. There was little doubt that they meant it when they said that they were going to be the new leaders in property service innovation.

By far the biggest change however was the absolute dedication to a high standard service culture. They really broke the mould of the old landlord/tenant relationship where the landlord basically provides as little as they can get away with, often communicating with the tenants through managing agents in a depersonalised and defensive manner.

At Tower 42 the tenants are customers and the whole emphasis is on delighting the customer with superb service over and above the terms of the agreement with a view to retaining their occupancy for many years.

One of the landmark decisions was to not to employ staff from the traditional area of facilities management, where they would arrive with all the old culture but instead to recruit from the world of five-star hotels where the service culture is strong.

Perhaps the easiest way to understand the changes that have taken place is to look at the service now provided within the complex that now comprises Tower 42:

- Reception service, smartly uniformed and speaking seven different languages.

- Concierge service, equivalent to a five-star hotel.

- Desk side tailoring service for suits, dressmaking and even footwear.

- Room service food provided by Wagamama restaurant sited in the complex.

- Private taxi service, exclusive to tenants.

- Health and fitness clubs offering different levels of gyms from 'New York boxing gym' to more conventional facilities, complete with pool, sauna, massage and health and beauty.

- Conference and private dining.

- Exclusive wine club with tasting sessions.

- Personal shopping service.

- Personnel services, including provision of trained and prepared temporary staff.

- Post room and reprographic services.

- Gary Rhodes restaurant 'Twenty Four'. Previously a dark grim brasserie that looked like a restaurant in an office block, now transformed into a destination venue, open for lunch and dinner and going for a Michelin star.

- Champagne and oyster bar 'Vertigo 42' – a destination venue, 600 ft above the ground, with stunning views across eight counties. Again a destination venue.

- Gourmet cookery club.

- Café Ritazza, utilising a former dead space on the ground floor.

- Dry cleaning.

- On-site mobile shiatsu.

- Complimentary internet and TV in the striking "club lounge" podium area.

- Telecoms and satellite TV.

- Inter-office netball and football leagues.

- Special events for occasions such as Halloween and Easter and a fantastic children's Christmas party.

- In-house training and personal development of a very high standard.

All of these are provided with style and panache. Whilst, naturally many of the services incur charges their provision comes at a cost to Tower 42 but the company believe the payback comes in the unusually high occupancy and renewal levels whilst maintaining a healthy rental income. The building is consistently 95% occupied and the policy is to always keep some capacity free so that they can accommodate existing customers with their expansion plans.

Of course, provision of services is one thing but delivering at a consistently high standard is quite another. Through their unique management style and passion for service they really do achieve this.

A great believer in 'moments of truth', Peter Merrett, the General Manager and his management team regularly review every aspect of their service. For most visitors the first impression is of the smart and exciting environment that greets you on arrival. The first personal interaction will almost certainly be at the concierge where the team led by 'Terry the ticket' greets you warmly and is always ready to help. 'Terry the ticket'? Terry, head of concierge takes his role seriously. He and his team are always smartly dressed in uniform with shoes sparkling. Dog walking, aspirins, private car-hire and theatre and concert tickets are all part of the service for Terry

In fact there is a true story told by one of the tenants, sorry, customers that sums up Terry's attitude. One morning he phoned Terry on his mobile, desperate for tickets that night for *Mama Mia*, a hot ticket at the time. "Fine" said Terry "I'll have them ready for you to pick up at the desk later this afternoon" Sure enough the tickets were waiting at the promised time. "Where's Terry?" asked the customer "I'd like to thank him." "Oh didn't he tell you?" replied the concierge. "Terry's in Israel on holiday, he was in his hotel shower when your call came".

A trademark of Tower 42's philosophy is that they do not just do things; they do them in great style and with real attention to detail. Take their temporary staff service provided by their HR department. For most companies, hiring a temp is at best a lottery but when you hire a temp from the Tower 42 personnel services, he or she comes uniformed, with a badge and a good working knowledge of the premises down to layout, services and fire drills etc. Furthermore they probably know how many sugars the directors like in their tea and coffee.

The service ethos at Tower 42 seems to extend to everyone you meet. Everyone is proud of the standards they achieve and clearly responds well to the challenge of providing excellence each and every time.

Astonishingly this is achieved despite the fact that Tower 42 actually only employs one person! That person is Peter, the General Manager. Everyone else is employed by one or other of the seventeen business partners who collectively provide the various services from engineering to hairdressing. But to meet them you would assume that they all work for the same organisation.

Tower 42 has been able to develop a real 'Team 42' attitude through a shared vision and mutual respect for all the players. Tower 42 spends heavily on training and development – paying, of course, to train and develop members of staff who do not work directly for them. The training executive, Jon Webb, trains and coaches all the team members including the 100 plus cleaners who are important members of the team, in customer service delivery. Jon is also a member of the Tower Action Group, a small senior executive team that constantly seeks to review service standards and drive improvements.

They hold the Investors in People accreditation, have been commended by the Metropolitan Police for their security vigilance (an essential activity in a city of London skyscrapers, following 9/11, but carried out with relaxed charm without compromising the activity) and carried off many awards apart from their successes in the National Customer Service Awards.

An outstanding example of the total buy-in of the staff comes from the chief engineer who was working at the building at the time that Tower 42 acquired it. From a traditional 'bogs and boilers' attitude to facilities management, he was sceptical at first about the new approach but is now one of the biggest advocates of the new regime and his gleaming boiler room never fails to impress visitors.

In common with many other service driven organisations, Tower 42 has a vision statement. Unlike many others however, theirs was produced by the staff rather than management. The statement reads:

> "We provide outstanding service and first-class facilities to exceed customer expectations. Our team is developed and encouraged to achieve the highest standards of excellence. WE LEAD, OTHERS FOLLOW"

To this they would add, "We do things our customers do not expect", "We do things that others do not" and "Near enough is not good enough".

No stone is left unturned in their search for excellence. Team members have travelled to New York, Toronto and Kuala Lumpur to study world-class facility management.

They meet with their tenants at regular feedback sessions, laying on refreshments and social activities so that everyone can get to know each other in an atmosphere of trust and relaxation.

As a result of their success, Tower 42 has expanded. Not by buying another tower block in a different part of town or in another city but acquiring sites in the immediate vicinity. They now provide services for five adjoining buildings creating a 'village of excellence' within the city.

The team at Tower 42 do not brag, but they love telling the story of their success and are proud to conduct a tour of the estate and without doubt they succeed

One might be tempted to wonder what lessons can be learned from the Tower 42 story? After all they work in a fairly specialised market, had a unique building and the advantage of starting with a, more or less, clean sheet.

First of all, they had the bravery to be really different and to break the mould in their industry.

Secondly, they followed through their vision consistently and persistently. They did not just pay lip service to their ideals but ensured that every action they took was congruent with the service they were committed to.

Next they cared about, involved and developed the team. They knew that customer service is more about great people than great facilities

Let's go to the pub for breakfast – The Engine Pub, Baldock

A Baldock pub has started serving breakfast to commuters. It's a refreshing business idea delivered with great service that's WOWed customer Colin Marvell.

Another winner has been nominated by Colin Marvell. Colin is worried about becoming a serial WOW! nominator (he also nominated

Lister Hospital). We're just happy he's looking out for the good stuff and telling us about it!

Here's what Colin had to say about The Engine Pub at Baldock in Hertfordshire:

"A transformation is taking place at a pub in Baldock. The new landlords, Dan and Sarah Cotterell-Clark, are turning a very average pub into something very special indeed.

The first signs of transformation took the shape of a pavement sign outside the pub asking 'Missed Breakfast? Breakfast rolls, Tea and coffee available 6.30 - 9.00am'.

Bearing in mind that Baldock station has never seen a newsagent or coffee outlet, it was a particularly welcome sight for commuters. To top that, a day later a further sign exclaimed 'free newspapers' (as well as early commuter breakfasts). I could not resist the lure of a free anything and ventured into The Engine at 7.30am the following morning!

Clutching an anonymous bag of fare and a take-away coffee, as well as my free broadsheet I ventured onto my usual train. It wasn't until I checked my change and the bag did I realise that, not only had I been undercharged but my bag contained not one but two of the bacon rolls I had ordered.

Not only did I get an unforgettable service memory from an unlikely source (at an unlikely time!) it was obvious Dan and Sarah had also thought very carefully about their target customers and consistently gone that extra mile to ensure that I went back, which, of course, I have.

We need more Wows just like this to prove to those visiting Americans who's really best at customer service."

I agree absolutely with you, Colin. This is a really nice example of thinking beyond the normal business boundaries. Given that they have all the facilities to provide some breakfast, why not make good use of them and attract some extra custom?

Game On! – Portobello Games

This is what customer, Stuart Bishop, told me:

Last year, I ordered their unusual toy 'Olive's Garden' for my eldest daughter for Xmas, after seeing it mentioned in a national paper.

It's a lovely toy for a craft-oriented kid, which lets them create their own 'garden in a box' with plastic flowers and foliage. Anyway, I ordered it on line, received it, gave it to a happy daughter - all perfectly efficient, and Alexandra is still happily playing with it now.

My nomination is after I received a package from Portobello yesterday in the post. I'll reproduce their letter in its entirety, and I think you'll soon get the point!

> "A while ago you were kind enough to buy Olive's Garden, perhaps for yourself, perhaps as a present, and we hope you were pleased with it.

> Recently we have been looking for ways to make Olive's Garden even better.

> We have introduced new flowerbeds, which look nicer and last longer. And we have added some delightful picket fences.

We would like our existing customers to have the chance to enjoy these new bits and pieces too, so we are sending you (for free!) a pack of each, and we hope you like them.

The new Olive's Garden is now in stock, just in time for Christmas. If you would like to place an order, do please visit our website, www.portobellogames.com the price remains the same - £19.99 plus p+p.

Thank you very much for being one of the pioneering Olive's Garden customers. We do hope it's given you as much fun as we've had making it.

Yours ever,

Lucy Baring
Portobello Games Ltd"

(and the absolute clincher for me - the letter is hand-signed!)

When a customer is offered something that might really appeal to them in such a personal way, is that great selling or is that great customer service?

I know what answer Stuart would give. And that's all that matters.

OWW! To WOW!

"Hands up! We got it wrong. Now let's see how we can get it right for you."

Here are some fabulous examples of businesses that didn't get it quite right...

at first!

Stockton-on-Tees Borough Council – Care For Your Area

In the year 2000, a Poll conducted by MORI in association with the "Independent on Sunday" declared Stockton-on-Tees as the second dirtiest town in Britain. Let us not worry about who was the dirtiest, penultimate position from the many hundreds of towns and cities in the country is not a place to be.

The newspaper carried the story and, of course, the locals were enraged. In that situation there were a number of reactions possible from the cleansing department. They could have said 'tough, that's how it is, we're a fairly deprived area and the job is extremely difficult'.

Or they could have partially addressed the situation and pulled up their performance to somewhere in the pack of 'also ran' towns. Stockton did neither of these, they literally took a new broom to the subject of cleansing and within years they became acclaimed as the most admired public cleansing department in the country.

One option that was not open to them was to throw money at the problem. Stockton, with an above average unemployment rate, is not a prosperous area and although the biggest impact on whether or not people are happy with their local council is street cleaning and refuse collection, the national agenda – to improve and invest in essential public services – laid down by the Prime Minister in 1998 set the investment priorities as Education and Health & Social Care. The result of this policy was that frontline services suffered and customer satisfaction with cleansing went down nationwide.

Stockton set about a remarkable transformation that involved considerable consultation, massive review of all procedures and practices, worker co-operation and support at all levels, imaginative thinking, strong leadership and a committed engagement with the community. They christened the new approach "Care for Your Area" and this slogan and accompanying logo is now synonymous with the cleansing department and their high standards.

The consultation process was particularly interesting and was instrumental in sending out the signal that they were really serious about change. They did not hide behind anonymous questionnaires pressed through letterboxes or left out in libraries. Instead they went out and met their customers by taking market stalls in each of the three market towns – Stockton, Teeside and Tayside – that comprise the Stockton-on-Tees Borough Council.

They also visited, mainly in the evenings, every single one of the 75 Resident Group meetings that they identified from town councils to parish councils and through to local estate resident associations.

Finally they conducted weekly telephone surveys and overall ensured that they gathered intelligence from all the users of their services: residents, businesses and visitors.

Not surprisingly, during this process, they took a lot of flak. The service was poor and the town was dirty. The locals did not need to read the 'Independent on Sunday' to know that. Although much of the information gleaned was already known to the authority, some useful suggestions and ideas emerged from these sessions. One item that came up time and again was the problem caused by missing refuse collections following bank holidays, the time it took to catch up and the problems that resulted from the delay.

Reviewing the situation, the service management team could see the problems facing them:

- They had a legacy of seven different outsourced contracts, with very little interaction between them. The result was that services were disparate and not conjoined.

- Budgets were overspent, with little control or planning

- There was a lack of performance management and general leadership.

- Customer feedback was damning.

- Very little recycling took place.

- Very little environment education.

- A lot of activity was being spent on 'fire fighting'.

- Worker morale was low and absenteeism was high.

- There was a lack of proper procedures and supervision. With a marked absence of written procedures and agreed standards.

- Finally the concept of customer care was completely alien to the cleansing team at all levels. It was a phrase used and applied elsewhere in the council services but did not, and could not possibly apply in cleansing and refuse services.

Solving the bank holiday problem proved to be a classic 'win/win' solution. Following consultation with the workforce and their union representatives, it was agreed to work a four day week instead of the traditional five days. This involved no additional costs and the same 37 working hour week. The staff was happy as they got a clear day off each week – Monday and the refuse collections could be worked to a Tuesday to Friday schedule with the loss of the regular disruption caused by the number of bank holidays falling on a Monday.

The results have been phenomenal. All of the measurements put into place show the continuing performance improvement but those are cold statistics for management and staff to ponder as they chart their progress but two accolades that stand out come from MORI themselves – the people that provided the impetus for change following their damning report in 2000 – and from the Audit Committee one year later.

MORI said just two years later in their 'The Rising Prominence of Liveability' report:

"……the biggest impact on whether or not people are happy with their local councils is street cleaning. It may be for this reason that ratings of local authorities have now fallen. Nationally, the **only** local authority that has gone against the tide in terms of local opinion is Stockton-on-Tees."

The Audit Commission awarded Stockton-on-Tees a rare three-star 'excellent' rating – the highest rating possible and the first, and to date, only time that it has been awarded for cleansing services saying:

"…..the borough was labelled one of the dirtiest in England and now it is one of the cleanest. The Council has a reliable rubbish collection and clean streets and public spaces. What's more the service has gone from average to outstanding in just 18 months. Street cleaning and waste collection may seem unglamorous, but they have a huge impact on people's quality of life."

The Stockton story is all the more remarkable when considering that cleansing is one of those customer service functions that can only go wrong! No-one congratulates the bin men when they collect the refuse each week but when they miss a week, everyone notices and complaints come pouring in.

The key to the transformation achieved at Stockton falls into two distinct headings, of equal importance:

Emphasis on performance management

and

Concentration on developing the skills and commitment of the people responsible for delivering the services.

They embarked upon a best value review, from which emerged a five year service improvement plan. With strong political leadership from the top and backed wholeheartedly by the chief executive and all the way down to operative level, the positive results began coming through within the first year.

On the performance management side, the challenge was to understand and document all of the tasks, agree standards and manage the performance to those standards. Ensuring that managers managed was an important part of the equation here as this had not always been the case in the past. A distinction was made between technical roles and management roles and appropriate training was delivered to ensure that the managers had the right skills.

Standards were set high but not beyond the capabilities of the staff who would be required to perform the tasks and providing enough time to perform extra duties such as answering the public in person when approached and either solving the problem on the spot or providing a calling card if the matter needed to be referred. Another matter that all cleansing staff can deal with, whilst going about their normal duties, is dealing with fly posting. The team has a 'zero tolerance' policy towards fly posting and each team member is equipped with a removal solution to attend immediately to the offending item, which is then passed on to the enforcement team who take the appropriate action.

With performance management at the heart of the new era, it is not surprising to see league tables showing latest weekly results, broken down by area, playing an important part in monitoring the success of the plan. Each week these are prominently displayed in the canteens as well as lying on the desks of the managers.

Also displayed in the canteens, alongside the league tables are the customer 'thank you' letters that arrive daily (and at over ten times the rate before 'Care For Your Area' was established.) Each person mentioned also receives a copy of the letter with a note from the Service Manager.

Of equal importance to the issue of performance management was people development. The human involvement in the work of the cleansing development, whether refuse collection, grass cutting in public areas or recycling waste, is huge. The work is labour intensive and needs caring and enthusiastic staff if it is to be performed to a high standard.

In reality, much of the work is relatively low paid and many of the members of staff involved have not come to their jobs through choice and design. In some cases educational standards are low and previous career histories would not make inspiring reading.

Before the new approach, the refuse team, for example, rarely saw a senior manager and unsurprisingly the relationship between the parties were distant and based on mutual suspicion. Once management started taking a real interest and managers were visible at the start and end of shifts, so gradually the barriers were broken down.

Now every member of the team, including the important refuse collectors, has regular appraisals and two-way communications are firmly established. Basic and specialist skills training is provided and there are many examples of previously uninterested staff now performing key roles, having undergone a personal transition prompted by the change in management attitude within the department.

The waste of human skills is one of the most serous crimes committed by management generally and Stockton rightly take great pride in their success at developing and utilising latent skills to the benefit of the individuals and the community.

Sickness rates, always a useful barometer of a successful operation, have fallen from some 25% to 6% - a great result in a work area where some health problems (such as back trouble) are inherent in the nature of the work.

All staff, including temporary staff used particularly in the horticultural side of the department, undergo the Council's induction training programme and the Care For Your Area specialised induction training, including health and safety issues (especially important in view of the equipment used) and the equally vital customer care issues.

A simple but very effective change was to maintain the front-line staff working in teams in their own areas. This has allowed the customers to get to know the individuals responsible for the important services they provide. In turn the team members take pride in their local areas and identify with the area. This, of course, enables matters to be dealt with in a friendly, constructive and efficient manner and is one of the main reasons for the change in attitude that has occurred.

The main result of the transformation can be seen with the evidence of one's own eyes. The street and parks and other common areas are clean and tidy with an absence of litter or fly posting. Once again there is real pride and belief in the area. Thanks largely to the work of all those involved in Care For Your Area, Stockton once again is a town where "dreams can be dreamed"

Accolades have been poured upon Care For Your Area and rightly so. The Audit Commission and the MORI commendations have already been referred to but wider based awards such as Northumberland in Bloom, the Cabinet Office's CharterMark and the Association of Public Sector Excellence and Investors in People provide further evidence of their total commitment to excellence.

Each one of these accolades provides not only ongoing evidence of success but an opportunity to spread the good news and to celebrate the success, always an important part of maintaining high level service performance.

As so often happens with outstanding organisations, they have achieved excellence not just within the obvious remit of their work but in associated areas where one would not necessarily expect the to excel. Their work in educating schoolchildren about environment issues, including litter and recycling has been outstanding. They produced a delightful book for primary schoolchildren "Meg and Molly" about the perils of litter whilst their Freda the Frog, recycling mascot has its own website and song.

With a caring presence throughout the town, they have even contributed to reducing crime through their work with local crime watch ventures and the Probation Service.

What lessons can be learnt from the remarkable story of service transformation at Stockton?

- The council certainly did not have huge budgets to throw at the solution. So the first thing to take from this case study is that dramatic service transformation can be achieved without large amounts of extra money.

- Consultation with customers is key to being able to meet and exceed their needs. Stockton's imaginative approach to getting out and about by canvassing views at market stalls in their Borough demonstrates that there are other ways to illicit opinion apart from the ubiquitous questionnaire.

- Thinking outside the box can produce outstanding results. The four day, same working hours week demonstrates this perfectly. Driven to find a solution, because it came up as a major problem from the consultation process, a simple solution was discovered that was always there whilst overtime and short-term increased workload initiatives were constantly failing.

- The importance of documented processes and performance management is essential to deliver high standards of service on a week-in, week-out basis.

- People are the most important element in delivering labour intensive services and their attitude can determine the perceived and actual success of the operation. To perform well, they need to be well regarded, trained, developed and appreciated.

How to say 'Sorry' – Sainsbury's, Stevenage and The Four Seasons Hotel, Bali

Businesses have a HUGE opportunity when faced with complaints. The majority of customers who have a complaint resolved to their satisfaction become more loyal after the event than they ever were before the problem arose.

Now don't use that as an excuse to make a mess of things for every customer. You'll soon get caught out. But, when things do go wrong, how can you win the customer round?

My first story is about my own experience at my local Sainsbury supermarket.

My wife, Maggie, had bought some fruit. But when she got it home we noticed that the grapes looked a bit 'manky' and the pineapple was past its sell by date. So I volunteered to take these back to the store.

Whenever I take something back I always feel a little apprehensive. I've got so used to people being defensive that I'm almost ready for a fight right from the start.

I went to the customer service desk and was delighted when the lady there offered to refund my money. No questions asked. Just a very friendly and polite, 'Sorry' and an offer to give me a full refund. She had exceeded my expectations.

But what came next was the icing on the cake.

She simply said, "If you would like to go and select some more grapes and pineapple from the shelf and bring them back to this desk, I'll let you have them free of charge."

WOW!

Empowerment!

This is what it's all about.

Lose the battle but win the war.

I estimate that we spend at least £20 per week on fruit. That's more than £1000 per year and we've been shopping in that store for almost 15 years. We've spent over £15,000 just on fruit.

We've probably spent more than £125,000 in that store in total including all our other food and petrol from their service station.

And yet I'm blown away by this gesture of just £3.98!

If you think that what Sainsbury's did was good then just read this story that Iain Grubb sent me:

> "My neighbours had just got married and went on their Honeymoon to Bali and stayed at the Four Seasons, the finest hotel on the island.
>
> As a special treat they booked the Honeymoon Suite. Upon arrival at the hotel they were informed that the Honeymoon Suite was double booked for the first two nights and so they would have to stay in a regular suite.
>
> The General Manager apologised profusely, but the couple was not only angry but also quite upset, as this was their honeymoon. The hotel offered a complimentary dinner, free excursions and bottles of champagne by way of apology. The couple went to their room still slightly upset but pleased with the way the hotel had reacted to the problem.
>
> On the second day the couple went on their excursion and returned to be informed that they could move to the honeymoon suite. They opened the door and looked into the luxury of the suite, the wife bursts into tears... why?
>
> On the bed, spelt out in rose petals, was the word 'SORRY'.
>
> This couple now recommends not just this specific hotel but Four Seasons Hotels anywhere in the world. This example demonstrates how going the extra mile can add to the

customer's experience, it would have cost the hotel nothing for the rose petals, but the impact on the customers was huge."

What can I say but 'WOW!'?

What's your system for turning a complaint into a magic moment?

John Lewis, High Wycombe

John Lewis has featured regularly in nominations for The WOW! Awards. Clive Wright had this to say:

"This is not the story of a small business, but I hope that it will not be overlooked for that reason. Big organisations can trigger the Wow! factor too.

Just over a year ago I set out to buy a computer, having very little knowledge of IT. When visiting shops I described my needs and spending limit. With the exception of John Lewis, everyone showed me computers with prices at, or above, my spending limit. Staff in John Lewis started with my need and, in fact, recommended something cheaper than I had expected to pay.

The model in question is a very well known brand. However, since I have owned it, I have experienced some problems and spent about £100 in premium rate phone calls to the manufacturer. Additionally, I had to send the computer away for repairs which took much longer than promised and in the process I lost all my data from the system.

I do not consider that John Lewis is in any way responsible for my problems, but I thought that I should write to them telling them of my difficulties, since the well known computer manufacturer provided no contact address. My reason for writing was simply to provide John Lewis with customer feedback and in the hope that they would forward my letter to the manufacturer. I did not expect, or seek, a reply.

I was very surprised to receive a phone call from a member of staff at John Lewis expressing great concern for my problems, even though I had made clear that I was pleased with the service provided by the store. What made this call more unusual was that I had not supplied my phone number. The person who called had already discussed the matter with staff in the computer department and told me that she was going to contact the manufacturer and make clear that they had fallen short in providing a quality service for a John Lewis customer.

I was even more surprised to receive, subsequently, a detailed letter from the Managing director, Mrs. Jill Lewis, expressing concern for my problems and offering to arrange for a member of her staff (a computer expert) to come to my home to help to sort out the minor problems that I was still experiencing. Since I do not think that John Lewis was in any way at fault, I did not take up this generous offer.

Mrs. Dewar apologised for the problem and described the service that I had received from the manufacturer as "appalling". No timid words here!

John Lewis is a large store, but the service that I received went well beyond the call of duty. Impressive too was the no nonsense, no excuse, approach. I was made to feel a valued customer.

I suspect that many assume that large organisations do not take the trouble to take a personal interest in customers. This is certainly not my experience of John Lewis in High Wycombe.

Of course, I am now much more inclined to shop at John Lewis and have told friends of my experience. No doubt the way that the managing director took a personal interest in my problem will be financially advantageous to the store in the long run."

Clive is absolutely right. Our expectation is that BIG businesses lack the personal touch. But this shouldn't be an excuse for any business. If John Lewis can find the magic formula then so can all the others.

Yorkshire Water – Most hated to most admired

In 2004 on April 1, Yorkshire Water was able to announce a remarkable breakthrough in water technology and production. They allowed the local radio station to announce that they had invented the first ever diet water "Yorkshire Water Lite" and that customers could apply to have a third tap to sit alongside "hot" and "cold" in their kitchens.

Water contains no calories but the company had developed a new process that resulted in H_2O with "negative calories". They received 5,000 enquiries for the new product by lunchtime when the radio station drew attention to the date (1st of April) upon which the announcement had been made. Despite this they received another 10,000 enquiries before the end of the day.

It was a publicity coup for Yorkshire Water and just one of a series of high profile initiatives undertaken to keep their name and the quality of their service and product at the front of their customers' minds. More importantly, that they have the confidence to indulge in some light hearted banter with their customers demonstrates how far they have come since the days went they were regarded as "the most hated" company.

Back in the late 1990s, if the matter was not so serious at the time, the public would have laughed at the company rather than laughing with them. It was true that the dry summer of 1995 had caused problems for all the water companies but Yorkshire Water's handling of the situation was exceptionally inept. They did not actually quite run dry – although they came close but they caused great alarm and despondency by the way they handled the communications as many of their customers were led to believe that they had.

The following year they were declared by a national newspaper as being one of the "most hated companies in the country". Not exactly an accolade designed to encourage staff morale and lift performance.

By 1998, the regulatory body OFWAT had them in bottom place (out of ten) in their customer service league table.

At the same time as all this was happening, other companies in all sectors of industry and commerce, were improving their customer service and Yorkshire Water's customers were saying "why not you?"

The company eventually got around to asking customers what they thought of the service and the results left no room for doubt about their feelings and the need to improve.

As if this was not enough the Government was constantly talking of introducing competition in all kinds of services that previously enjoyed a monopolistic existence and this thinking certainly included the provision of utilities.

If Yorkshire Water was to become a water supplier of choice, they would have to offer a very different service to their customers because in their current state very few, given a free choice, would have chosen them.

Finally, in his unfortunate scenario, they were on the brink of the toughest ever price review, with an immediate price reduction of 15%

being demanded by the regulator. This meant, in effect, the loss of one in five of the workforce.

Times were certainly challenging for the company who are the sixth largest water company in the world with 4.7m domestic customers and 140,000 businesses to serve. They generate £700m in revenue, employ some 2,000 staff plus many contractors, take over 2 million calls a year and carry out a million operational jobs each year.

With staff morale at an all time low, it was clear to management that something had to be done. They began by looking at what they wanted to become. What was their vision for the future?

They decided that despite the position from which they were beginning their journey that they wanted to:

"become known as the best water company in the country"

In effect they wanted to establish themselves as the supplier of choice by earning the loyalty of their customers as a result of exceeding their expectations at all times.

Naturally a starting point had to be asking the customers what they wanted. They developed an exhaustive customer consultation exercise known as "Voice of the Customer" – an exercise that has been regularly repeated since. Their future strategy was to be based on the findings from this exercise.

In fact, the customers' requirements were relatively straightforward. Above all else they wanted a reliable service but they were realistic enough to appreciate that things can go wrong. When this happens, they asked, resolve matters quickly and keep us informed, openly and honestly, about what is happening.

At this stage the company appreciated that this could only be truly achieved by an enterprise strategy that delivered consistent end-to-end process across the whole business. They also decided that customer service was not just the responsibility of a group of people sitting in a department that bore that name, but an activity involving everyone in the business including contractors and their staff.

In order to accomplish their mission, they realised that they needed a single and complete view of all interactions with customers and total visibility in real time of all work on the company's assets.

To do this they knew that they needed to invest in a new IT infrastructure as it was clear that their aging bespoke systems would not rise to the new demands. They set out to re-engineer their systems. By contrast to the existing systems they decided against a bespoke system but to utilise compatible systems that could do the tasks required.

More importantly, the project was not led by IT professionals but by those with operational and customer facing experience. Their main demands were:

- They wanted to be aware of all interactions with every customer. They therefore needed to log all customer contacts.

- To be able to give commitments to customers and be able to keep those commitments.

- To offer fixed appointments to all customers within a two hour timeframe. In other words not "we will be with you sometime on Wednesday" but "we will be with you between 10 a.m. and noon on Wednesday".

- They wanted customers to see the company taking the problem from the customer and owning it.

- After completion of the work, they wanted to make sure that the work has been carried out to the complete satisfaction of the customers.

With the outcomes in mind they set about building systems to meet their demands. The specifications of the various systems are outside the scope of this book but it is sufficient to record that they used 'best of breed, off-the-shelf' packages compatible with their platform systems and integrated the new systems, such as the contact centre system and the work management system with existing systems such as client billing.

Now they have really achieved the service levels that they were seeking. Just look at what happens when a customer contacts the company to enquire about services. Let's suppose the water pressure is low and subsequently only a dribble is coming through the tap.

The telephone call comes into the contact centre and straightaway the agent can tell from the name and postcode or the customer's reference number, exactly where the customer lives. The agent can then immediately access the water map of the area and can see if any work is being carried out in that area. For example it might be seen that there is some routine maintenance work being carried out nearby and that water levels will be restored within the hour.

If, however, it is a new problem, the agent can take the details and start the process that will result in a field visit and repair. All calls are logged and the case will be followed through until the job is completed and the customer is happy that the matter has been satisfactorily resolved.

Even more however, the agent when handling the initial call can tell from the map whether there are any further implications that might arise from the problem reported. For example are there any special cases in the area that might need alerting to the water shortage such as nursing homes, young mothers etc?

If an appointment is necessary, the agent can make it for the customer there and then, within the two-hour window described earlier. All future actions can be prioritised and the agent will have sufficient training to have asked the right questions so that any field visit will be by an engineer with the right technical skills to deal with the problem.

Currently 40% of calls are resolved at the contact centre and 60% of those requiring a field visit are resolved at the first call and incredibly 99.7% of appointments are kept on time. This is achieved in a working week, designed for the convenience of customers that stretches to a six day, 85 hour working week. Even where further and more complex work is required, often involving contractor staff, 98% of the work commences right on time.

Now let us look at the role of the field technicians. First of all they do not need to waste time by having to come into the office to receive instructions or file reports. He or she receives new jobs electronically via a "tough book" - a mobile and resilient PC that accompanies the field technician at all times.

Whilst on site the technician can access the water map, can report progress on the job (from "I am on my way" to job completed details). Furthermore all the technicians are customer service trained as well as being extremely competent engineers. To the public they are "Yorkshire Water in the field" and consequently have a high profile and many people's perception of the company is derived from their impression of the field technician.

In some cases the job may be allocated to a contractor and may involve some major work. The principles behind the service still do not change however. All contractors are signed up on long-term partnership contracts and subscribe to the company's customer service charter. The contractor has equal access to the water map and will report progress to the same standards as if Yorkshire Water itself carried out the work.

Whatever process has been involved in sorting out the problem, the contact centre agent is automatically prompted to contact the customer to ensure their satisfaction before the job is closed off.

The aim of Yorkshire Water is to engage emotionally with their customers. Having a problem with your stop tap may not naturally seem like a glamorous experience but the company really wants clients to enjoy their contacts with them. And curiously, they really do. In response to a survey 73% of customers who needed work carried out said that, despite the inconveniences that can arise, that they actually enjoyed the experience.

In the past, they found that whilst they were always good at engineering and fixing the problem, they were pretty hopeless at engaging with the customer and subsequently they were producing dissatisfied customers. They could just turn up unannounced, do the job and leave without anyone knowing. No one was satisfied, no one knew what was happening or when.

Let us look at the progress of a typical call today. A customer could ring to report a faulty stop tap. The next working day, at the very latest, an appointment will be made. Within the agreed time spot, the engineer will arrive and, even where the householder does not need to be present, the engineer will knock on the door to announce his arrival and explain what he is going to do.

When the job is complete, he will tell the householder and ensure that the customer is happy. It would not be unknown for a washer to be fixed on a tap whilst calling as an extra service. Finally, a field engineer will make a further telephone call to make sure that the customer is totally satisfied.

Again there are lessons that can be learned from Yorkshire Water

- First, when you are at the bottom, the only way is up. They did not fool themselves about their performance but took a good look at their position and planned their route.

- They were bold and ambitious. Instead of planning to be amongst the mix of water companies, from a position of being at the bottom, they planned to be "the most admired water company in the country" and when that aim looked close to realisation they changed the aim to becoming "the most admired utility company in the world."

- Bringing in contractors on a true partnership basis has led to a genuine 'end to end' excellent service record. How many organisations deliver good service themselves but are happy to blame external service providers, without realising that the customer does not care who is responsible, they just want the job done?

- IT can be an enabler for great service and it does not have to be of the expensive, bespoke, state of the art, cutting-edge kind. It needs to be right for the task.

- The customer service commitment is a journey not a destination. As Yorkshire Water has seen their plans come to fruition, they have set further goals and worked towards them.

Footnote: When it comes to appointments, Scottish Water can even beat the excellent record of Yorkshire Water, despite covering a huge area; they guarantee meeting appointments throughout Scotland within 30 minutes of the appointed time. One of their secrets is that when looking at this aspect of service, they thought, "Who are best at keeping appointments on time?" The answer they came up with was "Sales Professionals". Can you imagine a sales person saying to a prospective customer "I'll come by sometime next week, just keep your diary free for my arrival?" If they did they would get no business and they would soon be out of work. So Scottish Water got their field engineers to adopt the mindset and contact management of sales professionals when it comes to keeping their appointments.

Keeping Customers Informed – Flybe

Nominated by Richard Ward:

> "I was flying from Southampton to Jersey on Thursday 5th August on business- a regular trip for me. The flight was an hour late leaving, and when we reached Jersey the airport was fog bound. After three attempts to land the pilot decided it was too dangerous and headed back. After 10 minutes he came on the intercom to say that we were diverting to Exeter airport because we had a hydraulic fault.
>
> When we landed at Exeter we were met by a number of fire engines and asked to disembark on the runway away from the terminal for safety reasons.

Once in the terminal we were met by a number of Flybe staff. They went around ensuring that everyone was OK (some people obviously found the whole experience slightly traumatic).

After about ten minutes two guys bustled in and one jumped on the baggage carousel, announcing that he was Jim French, Managing Director of Flybe. He apologised for our inconvenience but stressed that passenger safety was paramount. He then went on to tell us that another aircraft would be available in about 90 minutes to ensure that we could continue our journey (with an option of return to Southampton for those that did not wish to), and said that refreshments would be laid on for us in the Boardroom.

This flight left on time and we arrived safe and sound in Jersey having been offered more complimentary food and drink whilst on board.

When I returned home the following evening there was a letter waiting for me from the Customer Services Manager at Flybe again apologising for the inconvenience caused. With this letter was a voucher for a free flight. Now that's what I call customer service."

When things start to go wrong it can be very tempting not to say anything to the customer. After all, we all hope that we might be able to remedy the situation quickly before the customer has even noticed that there is a problem.

What this nomination illustrates so clearly is how impressed customers are to be kept fully informed. Especially when they feel that the problem is being taken seriously by the senior management.

Sainsbury's' Bridge to Delight

It can't always be perfect. Life isn't like that. But this supermarket shows how to make a speedy recovery from disaster by putting the customer first.

Janet probably didn't know what she was letting herself in for when she volunteered to do the catering for a surprise 40th birthday party: 200 sausage rolls, 10 French sticks and 60 bridge rolls with a variety of fillings were just part of the order.

A visit to Sainsbury's Supermarket in Stevenage found most of the ingredients but Janet knew that the bridge rolls had to be fresh. To ensure there would be enough, Janet ordered them in advance. The order was carefully taken down by the assistant in the bakery department and would be ready for collection at 9.00 a.m. on Saturday morning.

Saturday came and party preparations were going well until Janet reached the bakery. The order had been lost and although there were plenty of French sticks on the shelves, there were no bridge rolls. Bridge rolls aren't even baked in that store: they are ordered specially from another store and delivered by van.

With the party plans collapsing, Janet started to panic and explained her problem to the bakery manager. The manager listened carefully to Janet's story and apologised profusely. No bridge rolls had been delivered, but the manager set off to try to find a solution with his team. Discussions were broken to ask when the rolls were needed and then resumed, with the team trying to find a way to get Janet her rolls by midday so that the guests could eat them at two o'clock.

When the manager returned, he made Janet a promise: "We will bake a special batch of bridge rolls for you and have them delivered to your home by 12 o'clock".

Janet was amazed at this and was about to leave the shop when she realised that she didn't know how much the rolls were going to cost. Or how was she going to pay for them when they were delivered. "Don't worry", said the bakery manager. "It's on the house because it was our fault."

At 11.40 a car pulls up outside Janet's house. Out gets a young man from Sainsbury's carrying two large bags. He apologises again for the mistake and hands over the bags of freshly baked rolls (still warm!). He goes on to explain that although Janet had only ordered 60 rolls, a batch run is 80 and so they gave Janet the extra 20 rolls as well.

Janet was thrilled: "The rolls were absolutely lovely - even better than the packs you would normally buy! The manager of the bakery was very helpful. He could have suggested that I make sandwiches instead. But no, he listened carefully to my problem, came up with a solution and delivered them on time and on budget! I recommend Sainsbury's for The WOW! Award".

Customer Service goes up in Smoke – St David's Bay Hotel, Cardiff

A Cardiff hotel went to great trouble to get a customer his favourite cigar.

Two team members demonstrated exceptional service at St David's Hotel & Spa.

Gavin Isle nominated St David's Hotel & Spa in Cardiff Bay, Wales to receive an award for the effort they expended catering for his needs while he was staying there.

"After my meal, I enquired about the availability of cigars. Whilst they had a reasonable selection, they didn't have my favourite brand, so I declined," says Gavin.

"Concerned about customer satisfaction and unknown to me, the waiter arranged for one of his colleagues to leave the hotel at 10pm in search of my brand of cigars. Less than 20 minutes later the waiter returned with two packets for me. Impressed, I asked where they had got them. Reluctantly the waiter confessed that the member of staff had gone to a garage three miles away to fetch them.

Both team members declined payment and a tip for their trouble."

Isn't it great to get such fantastic service and find that it's not just about making more sales – at least, not in the short term!

Like Your Carpets – Garden City Flooring, Letchworth Garden City

Garden City Flooring has been nominated by Melanie White.

"About two years ago this company replaced a number of carpets in my house, including the lobby, lounge, hallway, stairs and landing.

Recently, I noticed a few 'ripples' in the carpet. As they were not too bad, it took me another 6 months to get round to ringing them.

I called at about 4.30pm one day and was told by Liz, one of the owners, that her husband, Dave, would come round to have a look. At 6pm that same evening, Liz called me to ask if it would be OK for Dave to pop in at 8 a.m. the next morning. I was amazed at how quickly he was coming round.

The next morning he came and said he was concerned there may be a manufacturing fault with the carpet, but that he wouldn't know until his fitter, Alex, had pulled some of the carpet up to have a look. Dave asked when would be convenient for them to come round and I said most days after 4 p.m.

No further arrangements were made and I expected to receive a call in a couple of weeks when the fitter might have a gap in his schedule.

However, that same afternoon, at 4.15, Alex arrived to look at the carpet. He showed me the problem and told me it was a manufacturing fault, but that he could resolve the problem then and there. He carried out the work and told me that Liz would register a complaint with the manufacturer in case there were any more problems in the future. When the carpet was re-laid, it looked perfect again.

I assumed that was the end of the matter and was really impressed with the speed that Garden City Flooring had dealt with my problem.

Amazingly though, that was not the end. About two weeks later, I received a message from Liz saying that the manufacturer had agreed to replace all of the carpet affected - lobby, lounge, hallway, stairs and landing!

Very soon I had all of those carpets replaced with brand new carpet at no cost or inconvenience to myself.

I think that this is outstanding customer service as the company took it on itself to put a case forward for me with the manufacturer, without me even asking or expecting them to. Their service certainly far exceeded any expectations I had of them, and I would never hesitate to recommend them to anybody."

Once again, this is a fantastic story about recovery from a potential problem. Garden City Flooring has demonstrated that they are a company to be trusted. And when we are looking at potential suppliers, the one thing that we are looking for more than anything else is likely to be trust.

WOW!
that's what i call service!

Is this the conclusion or maybe just the start?

We consider ourselves very privileged to have worked with so many truly outstanding individuals and businesses.

We believe that standards of customer service in the United Kingdom have improved considerably since the mid 1990's. And we are delighted to have recognized some of those achievements through the National Customer Service Awards and The WOW! Awards.

So what can be gained from these stories of award winning businesses?

To start with, inspiration!

> We have been truly inspired by the achievements of so many individuals. And, from working with other organisations around the world, we know that the stories are inspiring people in all sorts of industries to give their customers better service.

When you look back through the chapter headings of this book you will see some of the key elements that we believe contribute towards outstanding customer service.

> Vision, leadership and communication are absolutely essential if a business is going to consistently deliver high standards of service. People need something to aim for. They want someone to follow. And the channels for communication, in every direction, need to be wide open.

> There is no question in our minds that the internal customer has to come first. Very few people go to work in the morning intending to do a bad job. The vast majority enjoys working hard and love to be recognised. And, let's face it; the largest proportion of our time is spent with our internal customers. When we give great service to our internal customers it ripples through in the service that they deliver to our external customers.

> Great internal service also has wonderful knock-on benefits in terms of reduced absenteeism and improved morale. We have to think about holding onto great people who work for us just as much as we think about holding onto customers.

> Empowerment is fundamental. Set the guidelines and the parameters. But let the people who represent your business, represent your business!

Possibly the greatest contribution of the National Customer Service Awards and The WOW! Awards is in changing the style of management within businesses. Both these award programmes focus on 'catching people doing things right'. Too much management time in the past has been spent on catching people doing things wrong. In the words of Bing Crosby, "we've got to accentuate the positive and eliminate the negative!"

The WOW! Awards is the only national customer service award programme based entirely on customer nominations. And we have been overwhelmed by customers' enthusiasm for this programme.

What we have discovered is that customers just like to say 'thank you' when they receive great service.

> Part of this is almost certainly down to the fact that they may have experienced poor service elsewhere and are now truly delighted to find a supplier that they can rely on.

> Part of it also is that customers want to be involved. When there is a formal channel that allows them to say, 'thank you,' then they understand that they are actively participating in the future development of that organisation.

> And finally, it would seem that customers give themselves a positive reassurance that they chose the right supplier in the first place.

> Businesses that do not open a formal channel together with processes for collecting customer praise, will only ever receive customer complaints!

Exceeding customer expectations is always likely to add the 'Wow' factor! Often these are only little things. But when they come as a complete surprise and can be delivered consistently they really get customers talking. Personal recommendation and word of mouth marketing have always been powerful factors in terms of business success. And the Internet is now taking this to new levels.

The Internet has also been a powerful factor in driving customer service standards higher. With so much information freely available to customers, about both products and suppliers, almost everything has been reduced to the level of a commodity. The only remaining opportunities to differentiate one supplier from another are in price and customer service.

Many of the basic principles of customer service were ignored for many years. It's more than 20 years since research established some of the key reasons why customers leave one supplier and favour another. The research has called it "perceived indifference" but we prefer to think of it as when somebody just doesn't care!

There were clear links established between customer retention and business profitability. Bain & Co discovered that a 5% improvement in customer retention could add at least 25% to the bottom line for most businesses. The Strategic Planning Institute discovered that businesses with good service records grew twice as quickly as those with poor service records.

And so what are those basics that were being ignored for such a long time?

Retention - simply understanding the business benefits of holding onto the customers that we already have. And also understanding how much more it costs to get a new customer that does to keep one that you already have.

Fulfilling promises - just do what you say you're going to do! It shouldn't be hard to under promise and over deliver, but so many businesses fall into the trap of making false promises.

Putting things right - simply respond to customer complaints quickly and efficiently. Business owners and managers always seem to be afraid of giving money back. And yet the reality is that in most cases all customers are looking for is an apology, an explanation and a reassurance that the problem won't happen again.

Moving from "OWW!" to "WOW!" Every problem, every complaint, every returned product is an opportunity; a gift from our customer! When we really exceed a complaining customer's expectations we create true loyalty, often even greater than before the complaint arose.

Our last piece of advice for everyone concerns taking action.

Change is the most difficult thing to instigate because it goes against all our basic survival instincts; don't leave the cave unless you have to, don't fight the lion unless you are attacked, don't hunt the buffalo unless you are hungry. And so it is easy to rationalise doing nothing.

The one thing that sets apart the people and business in this book is that they took action. They did something different. They stepped outside of their comfort zone. They took a chance. And in doing so they achieved something beyond their wildest dreams.

Go on. Go for it! Make your customers shout, "WOW! That's what I call service!"

Printed in the United Kingdom
by Lightning Source UK Ltd.
122717UK00001BA/9-24/A